David Marion   Dana Golden

ADDICTION RESCUE

THE NO-BS GUIDE TO RECOVERY

CONTENTS

Acknowledgements 1

Praise for Addiction Rescue...5

David's Note 7

Chapter 1 - Introduction to Addiction (Substance Use Disorder) 9

Chapter 2 - The Rules of Addiction 17

Chapter 3 - All Your Excuses 23

Chapter 4 - The Start.. 27

Chapter 5 - The Progression 31

Chapter 6 - The Beginning to The End 35

Chapter 7 - Getting Clean and Sober 41

Chapter 8 - Relapse and Cross-Addiction........................... 45

Chapter 9 - Consequences 53

Chapter 10 - The Elevator Analogy....................................... 65

Chapter 11 - Action #1: Wake Up and Pull Your Head Out Of Your Ass... 67

Chapter 12 - Action #2: Understand Your Addiction 69

Chapter 13 - Action #3: Find a Solution That's Right For You................. 75

Chapter 14 - Action #4: Do The Work 79

Chapter 15 - Action #5: Aftercare 83

Chapter 16 - A New Direction 93

Chapter 17 - Turning Your Life Around 95

Chapter 18 - Conceive 103

Chapter 19 - Believe 107

Chapter 20 - Achieve...111

Chapter 21 - You Are What You Eat 115

Chapter 22 - The Rules of Recovery.......................................119

Chapter 23 - Disrupting the Power of Obsessive Thinking 123

Chapter 24 - Finding My Redemption..125

Get Involved 133

About The Authors..135

Tear Out Sheets 139

Tear Sheet #1 Rules of Addiction 141

Tear Sheet #2 All Your Excuses 143

Tear Sheet #3 Rules of Recovery 145

Tear Sheet #4 Warning Signs of Relapse 147

Tear Sheet #5 Disrupting the Power of Obsessive Thinking.................149

References 151

Suggested Reading list 155

ACKNOWLEDGEMENTS

This is where we want to take the time to thank everyone who helped, encouraged, and gave us their time in creating this book. However, that list is endless, as the people we have encountered throughout our lives over the last half a century have contributed to the journey that got us here.

From David: I am overwhelmingly grateful for my family. My dad, although passed on now; my mom; and my brother and sister, who never gave up on me. There were times they didn't want anything to do with me, but they never quit loving me. Their examples gave me the will to keep trying. For Dana, who has stood by me even after divorce for twenty-eight years now, thank you for always believing in me and giving me hope. The gratitude I have for my two daughters is staggering. They got me through my darkest days. They are the light in my life that fuels everything I do. They give me the courage to be the man I want to be and are the reason everything I've gone through has been worth it.

I know this sounds crazy, but I want to thank the news media, government agencies, and investigators that brought me to my indictment and eventual incarceration. Without them I would probably be dead. As much as I despised them at the time, they saved my life and gave my kids their father back.

To all the sponsors, mentors, and sponsees I have had over the years, thank you for keeping my sobriety and abstinence in check. Thank you for letting me back in when I relapsed and never judging my journey. I am grateful for having found a higher power that has a plan for me I couldn't have possibly seen, that brought me through times of which I shouldn't have made it out alive, that gave me strength I didn't know I had, and that saw me through to the other side of addiction.

Thank you to my friends that have watched my journey and still call me their friend. Thank you to my prison mates that made three years of incarceration bearable. You are my friends for life. Thank you to all of you that encouraged me to get this book out there to share my experience, strength and hope to others in need.

Thank you to all those that have given me the opportunity to collaborate with you in my mission to help others into recovery and to find an end to the opioid crisis; Hazelden Betty Ford, Tonka Cares, The Steve Rummler Foundation, and Twin Cities PBS.

From Dana: Mom, thank you for your support and for believing in my abilities. You have always been there for me no matter how good or how treacherous my life has been. Thank you, Dad, for your entrepreneurial spirit and the hustle you vehemently showed me in doing what you have to do in life. Thank you to my big sis for setting the bar high, leading me by example, and letting me follow you around the country.

Thank you, David, for your encouragement when I had to take on being a single mom, running my own business, and getting our daughters emotionally and financially through high school and college while you were incarcerated. You showed me the way to understanding addiction, relapse, and recovery so I could write this book in an effort to spread our message and give others and their families hope.

Thank you to my beautiful daughters who have made all I do worthwhile. I would have given up long ago if your spirits hadn't given me what I needed to keep going. Thank you for being the amazing beings that you are that make me so proud to be your mom.

Thank you to my amazing group of friends that have been my support and family for my many years in Minnesota. Pattie, thank you for being my accountability partner while I wrote this book and your believing in me everyday.

Thank you, Bonnie, for your editing services in making this book complete. And even more importantly for your never-ending kind words of encouragement, not only as to what an important and timely book this is, but also for the job I've done in writing it.

PRAISE FOR
ADDICTION RESCUE

As a person committed to recovery, the co-owner of intense treatment programs, and having worked with thousands of individuals and family members, I believe it is critical to be honest with people about the stark nature of their disease since their lives are at stake. I appreciate the honesty that David Marion and Dana Golden share in their book, "Addiction Rescue: The NO-BS Guide to Recovery". David shares openly about the destruction he caused in his life and the lives of his family members while he was active in his addiction. He then gets into the solution and the transformation. He provides practical, real steps that I know work. Addicts, alcoholics and families who want a way out from the trap of addiction would benefit from reading this book.

– Albert Black, Recovery in the Pines and Spartan Recovery – Founder / CEO

After experiencing the loneliness, despair, hopelessness and anxiety associated with alcoholism, I was desperate to get help. I made the decision in 1997 to get honest with myself that I couldn't get sober on my own. I needed the direction and care of others and a Higher Power. Since that time, I discovered my calling, getting into service for others like me and their families. I've worked with thousands of individuals, hearing stories of their failed attempts at getting sober and seeing what has worked. I appreciate David and Dana's straightforward, honest approach in their book, "Addiction Rescue: The NO-BS Guide to Recovery." The book is an easy read of real solutions that can help others who are desperate like I was.

– Doug Dolan, Recovery in the Pines and Spartan Recovery – Co-Owner / COO

DAVID'S NOTE

I spent a lifetime making money to afford my drug and gambling addictions. That was, until age twenty-nine when my parents sent me on a one-way ticket to Minnesota to get clean and sober. I went from Wall Street stockbroker and sales manager in New York City to dishwasher at the Day By Day Cafe in St. Paul, Minnesota.

I left New York with the intention of getting a better handle on how to use drugs and gambling in my life. I quickly came to understand that using them, at all, was not an option. It only took two months for me to resign from my firm on Wall Street and settle into a different life in Minnesota.

I put my sobriety and abstinence first. I went to Alcoholic Anonymous meetings. I became a regular speaker at the treatment center where I was once a patient. I took my sales experience as a manager and trainer and became a motivational speaker in the areas of addiction and recovery. I helped as many addicts as I could to find recovery and sponsored countless guys.

And then I relapsed.

Everything I had once done for myself and taught others to do, I had abandoned. It would take me years to find my way back to recovery, and in the process I lost everything, including my freedom.

This book is a guide to my 5-Action Process, and "it works if you work it." (I borrowed that from AA.) But that's the bottom line: you have to work at it. Listen, if you're an addict or have someone in your life who is, you know how hard it is to work at that addiction. The time, money, attention, and thought that goes into being an addict shows just how hard we are willing to work at something. If there's a will to live a life free of addiction, there is a way. It's easy to do, but as I found out when I relapsed, it's easy *not* to do. And just as with any other job in life, it has to be worked to be successful.

My mission is to reach as many addicts as I can with this message of hope, and an easy-to-follow guide to recovery. And yes, I realize I said easy, yet I know there's nothing easy about kicking an addiction. Believe me when I tell you I've been through the worst of them. But with intention, persistence, and this 5-Action Process, you will learn recovery is attainable and a life free from addiction makes the work incredibly worthwhile.

My wish for you or your loved one is to find the happiness, success, serenity, and peace in recovery all addicts deserve. We are in this together. Addiction is a disease of loneliness and isolation, and—conversely—the answers are in the fellowship of one another. There is no doubt in my mind that by applying what you learn through reading and doing the exercises in this book, you can change your life in all the positive ways you've ever imagined.

I am always thrilled to hear from you if any questions, thoughts, or concerns come up along your journey through this book, or throughout recovery, so don't hesitate to reach out at anytime. I will always make an effort to get back to you within twenty-four hours.

David@TheLifeRecoveryCoach.com

So let's get started.

In life and recovery,
David Marion
The Life Recovery Coach

CHAPTER 1 -
INTRODUCTION TO ADDICTION
(SUBSTANCE USE DISORDER)

"In Essence, you make your choices, and then your choices make you."
- Darren Hardy

Today it's almost impossible to be unscathed by some kind of substance use disorder. Let's face it, there are workaholics, alcoholics, work out fanatics, gambling junkies, food bingers, social media compulsives, cigarette smokers, sex addicts, porn addicts, masturbation addicts, prescription pill abusers, illegal drugs users, love or relationship dependents, internet addicts, shopaholics, and video game obsessives. And there are so many other things that enslave us to their habits. They come at us from every direction, every angle, in every way, and they will never stop. If you're not afflicted by addiction, you're less than six degrees of separation from someone who is. You're either afflicted or affected; it's just a part of our society.

If you're questioning the numbers, let me share a few.

The Facts

Rehabs.com, a resource for addiction centers, states over sixteen million people have an alcohol addiction and that alcohol addiction accounts for approximately eighty-eight thousand deaths a year.

Origins Behavioral Health Care sites that 47.7 million people used mind-altering substances in 2017. Of those, thirty-six million used cocaine/crack or methamphetamine, thirty-six million used marijuana, and 18.9

million people misused prescriptions in the past year. The prescription class of drugs includes prescribed pain relievers (such as oxycodone), tranquilizers (such as Xanax), and sedatives (such as Valium).

The Centers for Disease Control (CDC) estimates that 72,287 people died from overdoses in 2017, an increase of about ten percent from the year before. That's 198 people a day. To get a visual of just how many people that is, think of an NFL football stadium. The average stadium holds just under seventy thousand people, so more people than a football stadium can hold die each year from overdose.

NBC Nightly News recently reported the chances of dying of an overdose are greater than dying in a car crash; one in every ninety-six overdoses versus one in every one hundred and three car crashes.

According to MediaKix out of Santa Monica, CA, internet and social media addictions continue to grow as our dependence on technology increases. Estimates show that over 210 million people suffer from internet and social media addictions worldwide.

The North American Foundation for Gambling Addiction Help reports approximately 2.6 percent of the U.S. population has some type of gambling issue. That adds up to nearly ten million people in the United States who struggle with a gambling habit.

The National Council on Sexual Addiction Compulsivity estimates that six to eight percent of Americans are sex addicts; that's eighteen million to twenty-four million people.

We're talking tens of millions of people. That's an incredible amount of people when there are only 325 million people in the U.S. Take into consideration *that* many people and then think about the millions of people in those millions of peoples' lives and you can start to picture how addiction has tentacles that easily reach most everyone in our society today.

Defining Addiction

I'm going to assume if you have picked up this book, you have come to or are in the process of coming to terms with the possibility that you have an addiction or know someone who does. If you are still questioning this possibility, let's talk about what an addiction is.

The definition of the word "addict," according to Merriam Webster, is "to devote or surrender (oneself) to something habitually or obsessively." In line with that, the definition of "addiction" is, "the quality or state of being addicted." That is the definition in its simplest term.

The American Society of Addiction Medicine (ASAM) gives a more in-depth look at the definition as follows, "Addiction is characterized by inability to consistently abstain, impairment in behavioral control, craving, diminished recognition of significant problems with one's behaviors and interpersonal relationships, and a dysfunctional emotional response. Like other chronic diseases, addiction often involves cycles of relapse and remission. Without treatment or engagement in recovery activities, addiction is progressive and can result in disability or premature death."

The ASAM also describes addiction as a brain reward system. The motivation to continue use is to recreate a memory in pursuit of the reward previously experienced. Those memories could be past exposure to such things as food, sex, alcohol, drugs, or other stimulations. Response to these external cues, in turn, triggers cravings or engagement in addictive behaviors. The reward structures of the brain are altered in an addict, and the motivation to use increases as the brain continues to adapt. The cravings for the memory, or reward, are relieved by substance use or other destructive actions. This dysfunction leads to characteristic biological, psychological, social, and spiritual manifestations in the addict.

As a professional in the field of addiction, I will give you my short take on it: addiction is any habitual behavior that causes stress and distress, and disrupts everyday life and relationships. It has no shut-off switch. It's a disease of being obsessed with more and more of whatever "it" may be. It's like being permanently hungry.

My Expertise

Let me tell you about me. I'm addicted, to everything. Oscar Wilde said it best, *"I can resist anything except temptation."* And I'm tempted by absolutely anything that makes me feel good. I've been addicted to everything from Rice Krispie bars to Heroin, hookers to slot machines. I've made tens of millions and gambled it all away. I lost my only wife to divorce and my two amazing daughters for a time. I've lived in penthouses, million dollar homes, and federal prison. I have paid my dues in the throes of addiction and as a felon, and I've come out the other side to find my redemption.

I'm a terrible addict, or I suppose you can say I am a very good addict. I'm textbook. If it's been done or said about addiction, I've done it or said it. I've been through it all, and I truly believe if I can kick the addiction beast, with the right information, anyone can. So, however close you are to addictive behaviors, whether in yourself or someone you love, there is hope, and I'm going to give it to you straight.

I'm an expert in addiction and recovery. I've been on one side or the other my entire life (or at least since I was nine.) I am a Nationally Certified Intervention Professional and a Nationally Certified Recovery Coach. I have spoken my message to tens of thousands of people around the country in the rooms of Alcoholics Anonymous, conventions, prisons, and schools. I've helped those in all walks of life and all ages, from kids in junior high school to old timers in Alcoholics Anonymous. I have sponsored hundreds in the AA program, and I am thrilled to bring my message to you.

This book addresses the addict but can help anyone who is affected by addiction. In this book, I show you the rules of addiction and what they require of an addict. I'm going to share with you what it takes to break those rules and to recover. It is not hard; it is not rocket science or brain surgery, but you will need an education and understanding to get it. It's easy to do, but it's easy not to do. Recovery isn't for everyone. If it were, for those who needed it, there'd be thirty million copies of this book sold already, Recovery is only for those who want it. You must be willing to do the things today that others won't, in order to have the life you want tomorrow. It's up to you.

I will warn you, I will be brutally honest, and I won't share in your sympathy, excuses, or blame game. I'm guessing you have enough people in your life who have done that for you already. If you're reading this, it's time to wake up and pull your head out of your ass. It's time to stop lying to yourself and those around you; you're just hurting them and yourself.

I will define for you the rules that addiction requires of you and the excuses you use to justify them. I will share my story from the beginnings of my addictions through the consequences they brought upon me. I am not, however, going to give you all the gory details of my life in this book; that, in and of itself, is a whole other book I intend to work on in the future. This book is for you to come to terms with and overcome the addictive behavior(s) in *your* life, whether the behavior is yours or someone else's. I will give you, however, enough of my background so that you understand I've been through the throes of multiple addictions. I'll also give you, for perspective, a reference point so you can see an example of how addiction plays out and the steps that need to be taken to recover from it. By sharing some of my story, I think you may identify with some of the characteristics we, as addicts, all share.

I will guide you through my 5-Action Process that shows how to get into recovery, how to turn your life around, and what will be required of you to stay there. I will address how to recover in body, mind, and spirit for the complete solution to living a life free from addiction.

I talk about journaling in Chapter 15, but I suggest you take out some paper (or a journal) and a pen before you read any further. As your read through the chapters, write down the things you can identify with, the similarities you find in yourself as I talk about addiction. You will find writing exercises consisting of reflective questions at the end of each chapter. These will give you an opportunity to check in with yourself, to see how addiction is playing out in your life and the role it is taking. Work on the answers to these questions; they will prompt you to start learning about yourself, giving you awareness and insight that can ultimately help you make the changes that you seek. Without this kind of awareness, change is not possible; after all, how can you change something you don't know exists? Take the questions seriously. Your answers will change your life.

You can also download the free E Work Book available at my website, TheLifeRecoveryCoach.com. This guide to the book has the writing exercises and the space to do them.

I also want you to pay close attention to the quotes you will read throughout the book; you will find them in italics. I have chosen each quote very specifically because of its significant meaning and value. Take the time to think about and understand them; they will bring you great insight if you do.

My wish for each and every addict is to find hope and to learn a different way of living.

Addiction is an obsession. The signs start when you think of nothing else but the next game, high, fix, deal at work, person, or whatever it might be for you. I don't care if it's once a year, once a month, daily, or hourly. It's an attitude and a fixation on the next one, of whatever it might be. It doesn't allow for balance in your life; it takes over the scale.

Your addiction is your mistress, your affair. (For some that may be literal, but for the rest of us it's a metaphor.) You are in a relationship with your addiction whether you want to admit it or not. And just as in any other relationship, you have a choice every day to stay in it or break up with it. It's time to take your life back, to stop letting your "mistress" have all the control. (Please don't take the word "mistress" as sexist or politically incorrect. It's simply a means to explain its power over you.) For simplistic purposes throughout this book let's call it "your fix of choice" or "addiction."

"Keep in mind that whatever you spend your time mentally attending to, that is what you are and what you will become."
- Dr. Joe Dispenza

And that says it all. Your thinking and obsessing about the next fix of choice is what you are and what you will become an addict of. Conversely, if you change your thinking and what you are obsessing about, you can change being or becoming an addict. So, let's change your thinking. And that starts with an understanding.

CHAPTER 2 –
THE RULES OF ADDICTION

"Addiction is an equal opportunity Destroyer."
- Anonymous

If you're not aware of how your addiction works in your life, I want to open your eyes to the fact that your addiction has certain requirements of you. Addiction comes with rules; they aren't printed anywhere for you to read about. Well, until now, that is. You can't readily notice them when you're in the throes of your addiction, and most likely, you're in denial that they even exist. But let me assure you, they do. If you don't believe me, run them by the people in your life; I guarantee they've seen you play by these rules.

> **Rule 1.** *Your addiction requires you to use the stuff (whatever that fix of choice is for you) whether it's killing you or the people around you.* The phrase "killing you" is not only in the literal sense of death (though it is an eventual fate much too often), Addiction kills physical health, mental health, spirit, finances, jobs, hopes, and dreams— all the good stuff life has to offer. Active addicts don't have relationships; they have hostages. Regardless of how much you are hurting yourself and those around you, your addiction tells you to keep going. It tricks you into thinking, "it's not that bad yet" and that you can quit at anytime it gets "really bad." But by the fact that you are reading this book, I'm guessing you can't.

> **Rule 2.** *Your addiction dictates where you hang out and who you hang out with.* You will find the places and people who support your

addictive behavior. Oftentimes when you're actually where you're supposed to be, you're most likely thinking about where your addiction wants you to be and who it wants you to be with.

Rule 3. *You cannot control it once you start.* If you are trying to control your fix of choice, I will tell you, you're already out of control. The one thing you have control over is the first one, that's it. The first one of whatever that fix is for you, you have control over it. After that, you have no control; your disease does. You control it or it controls you. There's a saying in AA, "When you dance with a gorilla, it's the gorilla that decides when to stop."

Rule 4. *You don't get to finish anything you start.* You might give a great 50-yard dash, but the race is one hundred yards long. You might give your best two years in college, but it takes four to get a degree. You might start a project, hobby, or job, but if your addiction is in control of you, it's likely you won't finish strong and even more likely you won't finish at all.

Rule 5. *Addiction kicks potential's ass.* I can't remember how many times throughout my life I heard how much potential I had. My teachers, coaches, and bosses all told me at some point along the way. But ten out of ten times, addiction kicks potential's ass. When addiction is in action, you can throw potential right out the window.

Rule 6. *Addiction is a selfish disease.* When addiction is running rampant, it's not possible to consider others and their feelings. This goes back to killing the people around you from Rule 1. It's virtually impossible to care for others when your disease keeps you from caring for yourself. Addicts tend to be self-centered and self-absorbed; it's the nature of the addiction business. Think of it as having a huge ego with an inferiority complex. Conversely, in recovery, I get to feel my best when I put others first; but active addiction doesn't allow for that.

Rule 7. *Addiction is a disease of loneliness and isolation.* Let's face it, when the most important thing on your mind is your next fix, it's hard to be present in any situation. My ex-wife used to say, "Even when David's around, he's not around." I might have been physically in the vicinity, but my mind was far away, isolating me from where I was and who I was with. I could be in a room with hundreds of people and still feel like the loneliest guy in the world. It's a disease of loneliness and isolation because it's all self-consuming.

Rule 8. *Addiction requires way too much space in your brain.* It keeps your mind trapped into thinking about the next fix. It's a mental obsession of the mind that manifests in a physical allergy and physiological condition. I like to say it's similar to a food allergy—I break out in spots when I use, but I never know where it will be: Las Vegas, Mexico, the Caribbean Islands, or even prison.

Rule 9. *Addiction will strip you of self-love and respect.* You also lose the love and respect of others, especially if you relapse and continue that vicious cycle. The shame and guilt of that can keep an addict stuck. Recovery is the antidote to shame and guilt. You can literally melt those feelings away as you overcome the self-loathing and disrespect that occurs as time in recovery accrues. Once you learn to care for and love yourself, you will be able to do the same for others. Self-love and respect are repairable.

Rule 10. *Addiction demands you do things you wouldn't otherwise do.* Addicts, to feed their addiction, will go to any lengths for the next fix. It has a 24/7, 365 days a year requirement of you that wants what it wants, when it wants it. It will make you lie, cheat, steal, and get up at all kinds of crazy hours of the night to serve its purpose. And it doesn't care who that upsets along the way. I can't count the times I've gotten up in the middle of the night to sneak out of the house to gamble because I was sure the slot machines had money in them for me. This is also called stinking thinking.

Rule 11. *Addiction makes you delusional.* If you weren't, you might just tell it to "Fuck Off." But it makes sure you never see how bad it really is or the hold it has on you. Think of it like walking around with your pants' zipper down and everyone but you can see it . Your disease keeps you in denial; it might even make you think everyone else has the problem and you're just "fine." If the people in your life are telling you your addictive behaviors are a problem, and you're the only one that doesn't see it that way, there might just be a problem.

Rule 12. *You'll never be able to get enough.* Your fix of choice will require you to use/do more and more over time. Addiction is a progressive disease; it holds you captive and demands more of you (explained further in Chapter 5). For non-addicts, moderation is an option, not so for addicts. As addicts, we can never get enough. When "normies," as non-addicts are called in the world of Alcoholics Anonymous, engage in a behavior such as drinking, they can limit themselves and perhaps never up their intake. Addicts, on the other hand, progressively need more and more, not having a shut-off valve. If you're not already, before you know it, you'll be drowning in your addiction.

Rule 13. *Addiction will hijack your body, mind, and spirit.* You will in time abandon all three. You will lose connection to everything but your fix of choice. In this book you will learn the path to getting back to all three, and once in balance, you will overcome your addiction. But do not be mistaken; you will have to do the work from the inside out.

Rule 14. *You will suffer severe consequences.* These negative consequences (I doubt I have to point out the word negative here; addiction has nothing positive to contribute) of addiction affect both the addict and those in the addict's life. All addicts experience consequences in some form; there is no escaping it. In time, your addiction will have ramifications on your health, wealth, relationships, job, dreams, and hopes.

Rule 15. *Addiction, left untreated, has one of three endings: jails, institutions, or death.* That's the reality of it. My addictions landed me in two of the three; I'm not willing to roll the dice in hopes of avoiding the third. For others, the bottom is six feet under. You have a decision to make as to where your bottom will be and how you want your story to end.

Looking at these rules, you can see how outright exhausting addiction is. Being addicted is a complete pain in the ass. I'm exhausted just thinking about what it used to be like. If you're not already, eventually you'll be sick and tired of being sick and tired.

You're going to have to break these rules if you want to recover from your addiction. I'm sure you're used to breaking all kinds of rules, but it's time to show your addiction who's boss and kick its ass.

CHAPTER 3 -
ALL YOUR EXCUSES

"Excuses are the nails to build a house of failure."
- Jim Rohn

et's go over some of the common excuses addicts use for themselves and the people around them. These are the justification modules that we, as addicts, sell ourselves on to continue our addictive behaviors. If you're an addict, I'm guessing you've probably used one or more of these from time to time and more likely, most of these, most of the time. I know I did, lots. I'll also say these are probably some of the same things you're in denial about, the things that keep you stuck. So I suggest, right about now, getting honest with yourself. As you read through these, make notes about which ones you've used and how they apply in your life.

1. *If it gets really bad, I'll quit.* I can't begin to count how many times I told myself this as well as anyone else that had a problem with my addiction.

2. *Everyone else does it.* The thing is, "everyone else" may not be an addict. You have to get over the fact that you just might not be able to do things other people can.

3. *You'd do it, too, if you had my life.* From a horrible boss to a nagging spouse, we try to convince ourselves, and others, our life is just too unbearable to live without our addiction. But since we are the only ones in control of our lives, it is up to us to change the circumstances that cause the destructive behavior(s). For instance, if

drinking is your addiction, and a horrible boss is your problem, better to get a new job than stay in one that's causing you to poison yourself with alcohol.

4. *I'm more interesting and outgoing when I do.* This was my very first excuse when I started drinking at age thirteen. I went from shy introvert to fun extrovert. I felt I finally fit in once I found alcohol and drugs. Oftentimes, our fix of choice makes us comfortable in our own skin for the first time.

5. *I'm not hurting anyone.* Oh boy, if you only knew. As addicts, we are so focused on us we can't see outside ourselves. We truly believe we're only hurting ourselves, if anyone at all. We are in complete denial about destroying the lives around us.

6. *No one understands me or can help me.* Addicts feel isolated and alone. We believe we are terminally unique and no one can possibly understand us and therefore help us. We would rather keep our addictions as well as the thoughts that go along with them to ourselves.

7. *I'm never going to amount to anything anyway.* Addiction destroys self worth, self-confidence, and self esteem. The spiraling down effect that addiction causes leaves addicts without the ability to see any means to bettering themselves, and therefore they see no way out at all.

8. *This is who I am, and I'm ok with it.* Because addicts lose their power over their addictions, they come to terms with thinking the addiction is who they are. Because they don't see a life without their addiction in it, they convince themselves it's ok. In reality, though addiction is always a part of the addict, (as I say, it's called alcoholism not alcoholwasm) it does not have to be active, define one's life, or have control over the addict.

9. *I can stop whenever I want.* As addicts, we are in denial, thinking we have control over our disease. We like to see it as something we

choose to do, not have to do. Therefore, we are in constant belief that we can stop anytime we choose to. Unfortunately, as any addict that has tried to stop will tell you, the will to stop has no power over our addiction's hold on us. Often the addict believes they don't have an addiction, but rather just overuse or abuse.

10. *I deserve this escape.* Unrelenting jobs, raising kids, hectic schedules, and other pressuring life circumstances give an addict this excuse to engage in their addictive behavior. Using, in whatever form the addict chooses as an escape, is not dealing with their life, but rather letting their addiction make their choices.

11. *I've always been the black sheep of my family.* Being different and not fitting in are strong arguments for addicts to use. When we think of ourselves as inferior to others, we lack the self-esteem to make superior choices for our own selves. This excuse perpetuates itself when our fix of choice gives us a sense of fitting in or belonging.

12. *It makes me better/happier.* This is another excuse I used all the time. Being an athletic guy, I could have sworn that using drugs and alcohol made me better at sports. Or how about this one: I have a friend who used to say she was a better driver when she drank because it was the only time she actually paid attention to the speed limits and her driving. I thought, for years, I was happier when I was high, but I now know that was just my addiction's way of keeping my attention.

13. *I'm not as bad as him/her; now they have a problem!* There will always be someone to compare yourself to in any area of life. Trying to find an addict that "has it worse" than you is a futile exercise. Everyone has a different capacity for their addiction and a different bottom. The consequences you suffer are yours; it doesn't matter what someone else's are. What matters is your life and what's happening in it. Justifying your use by thinking it's not as bad as someone else's is just another sign of denial.

14. *I'm not suffering any earth-shattering consequences.* Maybe not yet, but you will. It might start with the loss of your wallet or a friend. It might escalate to a spouse or a child or result in a serious health risk or accident, but in the end, left uncared for, your addiction will lead you to jail, an institution, or a grave.

15. *I don't do "it" (whatever your fix is) that much.* If you have to justify your behavior by using these words, chances are you're doing "it" too much. What's "that" much anyway? If this is your response to your behavior, I can guarantee "that much" is too much whether it seems like it or not to you.

16. *I only do it on the weekends.* For now. But, in time, because of the progression of the disease, you will find yourself making excuses on a Thursday or for happy hour or a social event on a Wednesday. It will escalate, and it won't just be on weekends in the end.

17. *I don't go at it hard-core or use the hard-core stuff.* If you're someone that thinks you have it under control because you only drink beer and not liquor, only smoke weed and not crack, only watch porn but haven't had an affair, think again. It's not a matter of what the stuff is; it's the attitude and behavior that goes along with it.

18. *The universe is always conspiring against me.* If you're a person who thinks this, then you have a negative attitude. If you look for things to prove this, you will consistently find them. Likewise, if you think the universe is always conspiring with you, you will find proof in this. By having this negative attitude, you are perpetuating things going wrong in your life, and as we will discuss later, the universe is always giving you what you ask for. Like it's said, "Be careful what you ask for" because that's exactly what you are getting at any given time.

CHAPTER 4 –
THE START

"Your background and circumstances may have influenced who you are, but you are responsible for who you become."
- Darren Hardy

Every addict has a story. Some are stories of broken households inundated with violence, drugs, government assistance, and crime. Others are stories of upper-class families with white picket fences, summer vacations, and private schools. It doesn't matter where you start because addiction doesn't discriminate; it provides an equal opportunity for all.

I'm a Jewish kid from New York, born in 1959. I grew up middle class in a very "normal" family. It became apparent fairly early on, however, I was not normal. I did not have the same interests as my older brother or younger sister, nor was I fitting in with the kids my age. I guess you could say I was the black sheep in my family. (Excuse 11. I've always been the black sheep of my family)

At nine years old, I found my herd of others who didn't identify with their peers either, and with them, I started gambling. While most kids my age were at the movies, playing football, or trading baseball cards, I was playing poker for money on Friday and Saturday nights.

We all were given nicknames; the regulars where Whitey, Pickles, Little Dort, Fudd, Imma, and I was Emmis. Emmis became my first nickname and gambling my first addiction. I thought all week long about the next weekend and couldn't wait to go at it again. It was what I lived for. I was hooked before I knew what it meant to be hooked; I just knew I couldn't get enough. (Rules of Addiction #3. You cannot control it once you start.)

Because the disease of addiction progresses, as talked about in Rules of Addiction #12, you will have to use/do more and more over time, had I known what to look for, I could have watched it play out in my life. It was that apparent.

As I got older and into my teens, I found pot and alcohol and felt I fit in much better because of them. They became habits that made me feel more alive, confident, and likeable. They gave me the mask I needed to be comfortable in my own skin. I was under the impression that drugs and alcohol were making me a better, happier kid. They made social situations easier to handle. I had more friends, was invited out more often, and was able to have more fun being comfortable with myself and around others. Clearly, in my mind, life had gotten better. (Excuse #4. I'm more interesting and outgoing when I do. Excuse #12. It makes me better/happier.)

I would learn later I was misguided in that assumption.

Turns out I was a good athlete, and I played basketball, baseball, and soccer in high school. I never quite fit in with the jocks, though, opting for the misfits instead. Unlike myself, the real jocks were committed to their sport and anxiously anticipated the next game day. I suppose it was their way of feeling good—points, scoring, or accolades from their peers or parents. The only things that made me feel good were drugs and alcohol. I was only obsessed with my next fix, not the next game, and couldn't have cared less what anyone thought. I would later learn addiction is a selfish disease, and though I didn't know that at the time, I was already living it. (Rules of Addiction #6. Addiction is a selfish disease. Rules of Addiction #8. Addiction requires too much space in your brain.)

I got fired from my first job at Dunkin Donuts for drinking on the job; I was fifteen. I got my second nickname when my friends dubbed me Dunkin Dave on the way in, and my third, Drunken Dave, on the way out. I was already suffering consequences from my addiction. (Rules of Addiction #4. You don't get to finish anything you start.)

For me, addiction started early, as if I came out of the womb with a genetic predisposition to become obsessively hooked on things that gave me pleasure.

The Facts

According to the U.S. Library of Medicine, kids of addicts are eight times more likely to be addicts themselves. This genetic predisposition is what is commonly referred to as an addictive personality. My father, though never talked about, had a gambling problem, and I have an aunt who's been in recovery for twenty-four years. I'm going to assume my genetic predisposition gave me my start.

For others, the other fifty percent who are not genetically predisposed, the U.S. Library of Medicine again tells us, it's a lack of coping skills, and it can show up anytime. There could be a trigger, an event or emotion that sets the course. It can be the environment you grow up in, the people you surround yourself with, your parents, friends or siblings. But if you're experiencing some form of addiction in your life, it doesn't really matter which fifty percent you came from, genetically predisposed or a lack of coping skills. You're just in.

There are traits of an addictive personality that can be spotted early on. Had someone been looking for them in me, they would've have seen them as early as nine years of age. Some of the traits that expose themselves initially are: a love of excitement, the need for more to get the same thrill, impulsivity, inability to quit, and engagement in high risk activities.

For those that become addicted because of a lack of coping skills, the causes are most likely associated with stress, anxiety, depression, or negative thinking. These conditions are red flags that can lead to addiction susceptibility. The Fix, a resource for addiction and recovery, says anxiety, depression, social alienation, emotional avoidance, and risk-taking behaviors can be indicators a teen is extra-vulnerable to addiction.

None of these conditions are a determination that addiction will follow, but they are warning signs to be taken seriously. The National Survey on Drug Use and Health (2017) indicates that some children are already abusing drugs at age twelve or thirteen, which likely means that some begin even earlier. Early abuse often includes such substances as tobacco, alcohol, inhalants, marijuana, and prescription drugs such as sleeping pills and anti-anxiety medicines.

However it starts, it can be attributed to the pleasure-seeking nature we as humans are born with. It is natural that we pursue things we enjoy; things such as good food, a tasty cocktail, or a fun activity can make us feel good. A healthy, non-addictive brain can store the good feeling away and move on with life, while an addictive personality gets stuck on it. For the addictive personality, it's when those things become a fix for something we are missing, for example: relationships, friends, self-esteem, self-respect, confidence, or self-worth. It becomes a way to self-medicate. In the case where using is due to a lack of coping skills, it becomes a problem that often turns into an addiction. (Rules of Addiction #9. Addiction will strip you of self-love and respect.)

Writing Exercise

- [ ] *Do you come from a family with addiction issues?*

- [ ] *If so, what kinds of behavior did you witness?*

- [ ] *Did you come into your fix of choice due to circumstances or environment?*

- [ ] *If so, who or what was the influence for you (an event, person, emotion)?*

- [ ] *When and what are your first memories of not being able to get enough of something?*

- [ ] *What is your fix of choice fixing for you (think about what's missing)?*

CHAPTER 5 -
THE PROGRESSION

"Addiction takes you to Hell, disguised as Heaven."
- Unknown

It was 1977, and somehow I managed to graduate high school, but as Rules of Addiction #4 states, I sure wasn't able to finish strong. That being the case, I didn't have many options for college; my best offer was to stay local, and I went to The State University of New York in New Paltz. (Rules of Addiction #4. You don't get to finish anything you start. Rules of Addiction #5. Addiction kicks potentials ass.)

I spent my time there trying to keep college life together while doing any drug I was introduced to. Experiencing new kinds of highs became an addiction in and of itself. Quaaludes became my new fix of choice, and I spent the rest of my time in New Paltz getting my hands on as many as I could. (Rules of Addiction #12. Your fix of choice will require you to use/do more and more over time.)

After two years, I was able to transfer schools, and I opted for the nicer weather in Tampa, FL. The University of South Florida (USF) was the only Florida school that would take me; that was fine with me.

I got to Florida in 1980 with the resolve to start over and do better at school and life. I was going to take my classes seriously, and I walked onto the Division 1 basketball team at USF. By showing up on the court every-day and working hard, I earned myself a spot on the practice team. I had slowed down my partying, was making better grades, and had gotten myself back in good physical condition. (Rules of Addiction #3. You can't control it once you start.)

I also trained in karate. I met an instructor who gave me a free membership in trade for cleaning the dojo. Andre was a lethal weapon as a fifth-degree black belt, and training under him was a privilege. I'd spend hours there and moved through the ranks in testing for my belts. I started competing and winning statewide competitions, eventually taking one third place and three first place wins in national competitions.

Ultimately, this too, came to an end. Although I was trying to do all the right things, my addictions were pulling on me more and more, and I gravitated to people and places to feed them. Cocaine was everywhere, and it didn't take me long to find my new fix of choice. I replaced my time in the dojo with a job as the head doorman at Zapps, a nightclub in Tampa where I could more easily justify my using. (Rules of Addiction #5. Addiction kicks potentials ass. Rules of Addiction #2. Your addiction dictates where you hang out and who you hang out with.)

Florida was a haven for bikini clad coeds and endless parties with beautiful sunrises, which I saw all too many of. Right about the time I could test for my black belt, I gave up karate. Soon after, I was kicked off the basketball team due to my irresponsible behavior on the court or, at times, not showing up to practice at all. I would miss semesters of school at a time due to my lack of interest, and it took me seven years to graduate. (Rules of Addiction #4. You don't get to finish anything you start.)

After graduation, I moved back to New York, and a friend of mine lined up an interview for me with his firm on Wall Street to be a stockbroker. I went in with a nothing to lose and everything to gain attitude, and when the partner I was interviewing with asked me where I saw myself in five years, I told him behind his desk telling him what to do. I got the job.

It was the mid 80's on Wall Street, and it was booming and exciting. I made more money than I could have imagined, lived in a penthouse in the city, and snorted more cocaine than I would have thought possible.

(Rules of Addiction #12. Your fix of choice will require you to use/do more and more over time.)

Within six months, I was invited, along with four other brokers and the partners of the firm, to attend a conference in Chicago. When I asked the partner that had invited me, "Why me?" he told me they had never seen anyone come into the business with the potential I was exuding. (Rules of Addiction #5. Addiction kicks potentials ass.)

We flew to Chicago on the company plane, and not long into the flight, one of the managing partners put something unfamiliar in my hand and said, "Here son, go in the bathroom and take care of yourself." I promptly got up, went into the bathroom, locked the door, and unfolded my hand to find an ornate gold canister full of cocaine. I snorted as much as I could without taking an unreasonable amount of time in the bathroom, looked in the mirror, adjusted my tie, and said aloud to myself, "Congratulations, you've made it." (Rules of Addiction #11. Addiction makes you delusional.)

I was sure this was success. In reality, it was the beginning to my end.

Things I had started out enjoying—sports, people, even gambling as a kid—lost their luster as my drug use escalated. With each new found fix, each time I chased the previous high, everything else going on in my life suffered through neglect. (Rules of Addiction #7. Addiction is a disease of loneliness and isolation.)

There would be dozens more examples of how this played out in my life, not just sports but jobs, relationships, even my addictions—whether a different drug, a different game to gamble on, or faster way to make money. I couldn't get enough of whatever the fix was at the time and continually looked for the next best fix. And, in direct proportion, as each intensified, I paid less and less attention to the other aspects of my life. I would later learn how important it is to keep all areas of life in balance. When I was in the depths of using, I wasn't capable of mentally checking in with my life. (Rules of Addiction #6. Addiction is a selfish disease.)

The Facts

As an addict, it makes sense that as our disease progresses, our interest in everything else diminishes. Addictions never level out. Because it becomes harder for us to reach the same level of satisfaction, we need to engage in addictive behaviors more and more often. Even when we are unsatisfied or no longer enjoy the addiction, we are in constant hope to achieve the level of pleasure we once did. (Rules of Addiction #12. Your fix of choice will require you to use/do more and more over time.)

As our brain continues seeking more reward stimulus—the ever-elusive high we are increasingly chasing—it suppresses our ability to focus on the other things we once enjoyed. These can include people, places, things, hobbies, work, and the like. Apathy creeps into all areas of our life, and the only thing that excites us is our next fix.

Writing Exercise

- [ ] *When did your fix of choice escalate?*

- [ ] *What other fixes of choice became your next obsession?*

- [ ] *What things did you not finish strong or finish at all because your fix got in the way?*

- [ ] *What consequences were you experiencing along the way?*

- [ ] *What were the people around you noticing?*

- [ ] *What places and people in your life were dictated by your fix of choice?*

- [ ] *What things did you trade in for your fix of choice?*

CHAPTER 6 –
THE BEGINNING TO THE END

"If you want to start feeling good about yourself,
stop doing the things that make you feel bad."
- David Marion

I was out of control. I drank all night in clubs and did cocaine all day to stay awake. The hookers and coke whores came and went, as did the drug dealers. It was a circus, and not the kind that's family friendly. I became estranged from everyone close to me; I surrounded myself with only those who validated my behavior. (Rules of Addiction #2. Your addiction dictates where you hang out and who you hang out with. Rules of Addiction #7. Addiction is a disease of loneliness and isolation.)

A co-worker suggested I try to slow down, take it easy. My lifestyle was catching up to me, and I was showing the wear. My behavior had gotten aggressive and moody; I didn't like the way I felt, and I took it out on everyone else. I had risen to a sales manager position on Wall Street, and I constantly yelled at and berated the other brokers. I jumped on desktops and slammed phones while I held sales meetings. I was an asshole. (Rules of Addiction #9. Addiction will strip you of self-love and respect.)

It was suggested I try an AA meeting.

I'll never forget my first meeting. It was held on a Friday night on 79th Street and 1st Avenue. An old-timer in the program made me stand in front of the group of forty to fifty people, handed me a 24-hour medallion, and said, "Son, I have good news and bad news for you. The good news is you no longer have to drink the stuff, smoke that shit, or snort anymore because we found a common solution to recovery."

I asked, "That's great, but what's the bad news?" He answered, "The bad news is, take a look around this room because we're going to be your new best friends," and he gave a hearty laugh. I took a good look around the room and realized I wanted nothing to do with these people. A bunch of drunks, young and old, drinking coffee, smoking cigarettes, laughing, and hugging each other; this was not my tribe. I knew this wasn't for me. I left and got high.

I thought I knew what success looked like, and it was a lot like Wall Street. I would have bet the farm that it was about the suit I was wearing, the amount of money I had in my pocket, what the girl on my arm looked like, or the kind of car I was driving. See, I had always thought success was an outside job. I would later learn the term for this; it's called other-esteem. As I talked about in the Rules of Addiction, addicts lack self-esteem and self worth; therefore, we look for things outside ourselves to fill us up, to give us self-assurance and confidence. This is not a healthy form of esteem.

In my delusion, I had nothing in common with the people in that AA group. There's a good chance someone in that room had answers for me, but I was too attached to my ideas of what successful people looked like to be open to it. It would take me years to understand what success really looked like. That it's an inside job and has nothing to do with what's happening on the outside.

The people I was judging at that AA meeting were experiencing success right in front of me, but I was too ignorant to have possibly realized it at the time.

Here's something to consider, something I learned later, and would come to use as a measuring stick in my life: Earl Nightingale's version of success. In 1957,he said this about success, "The only person that succeeds is the person who is progressively realizing a worthy ideal. It's the person that says I'm going to become this and then begins to work towards that goal. Success is anyone who is doing deliberately, a predetermined job because that's what he decided to do, deliberately."

There was nothing in my life I was doing deliberately. Everything I was doing was by happenstance. I had no goals, no vision for my future. I wasn't working towards anything. Certainly not a worthy goal, even if you consider the money I was making, the penthouse I was living in, or the clothes I was wearing; these were not "worthy" goals. And certainly the destruction I was causing to myself physically, mentally, and spiritually was not deliberate. I was barely surviving; nothing in my life was thriving other than my addictions.

I couldn't remember the last time I had been sober or had been around sober people (other than work). I couldn't stand the vicious cycle that my life had become. Everything I thought would make me happy had turned miserable. I didn't know how to make it stop. I had one foot out my twenty-first floor penthouse apartment window when I called a dear friend from high school. For the first time, I got honest about my using and shared with her I couldn't go on.

It had gotten really bad, and I had no idea how to quit.

My high school friend called my parents, and the next thing I knew, they were all in my apartment for an intervention. I was given a one-way ticket to a treatment center in Minnesota and a ride back to my parents where I would stay for the two weeks before the facility could get me in. I spent those two weeks as if I was a binge eater about to have gastric bypass surgery. I did as many drugs as I could, being damn sure to get my fill before the party was over, literally. . (Rules of Addiction #15. Addiction, left untreated, has one of three outcomes: jails, institutions, or death.)

For every addict, the beginning to their end shows up at a different place and time in their addiction. It's the crossing of a line when the fix becomes an addiction, the addiction becomes an obsession, and the obsession becomes a downward spiral that cannot be stopped. For some it happens with the first use, and for others it grows out of time spent on the addiction or the amount of use.

Here are some ideas to consider in identifying your beginning to your end.

- When others stop and you cannot.
- When you stay behind to finish someone else's.
- When others are ready to go home and you are not.
- When you don't want the situation to end.
- When you feel like you can't get enough of your fix of choice.
- When you need more and more to feel the same amount of pleasure.
- When you spend the majority of your time thinking about or doing the behavior.
- When you become dependent on the behavior to handle emotions or to feel "normal."
- When you continue the behavior regardless of experiencing physical or mental harm.
- When you have trouble cutting back even when you want to.
- When you neglect other areas of your life to continue the using behavior.
- When you minimize or hide the extent of your behavior.
- When you experience withdrawal symptoms when trying to stop or cut back (physical pain, irritability, or depression).

If you experience one or more of these things, it is likely you have crossed the line and addiction has crept into your life. You've already begun. Only you have control over where and when it will end.

There is a myth attached to addiction that one has to hit "rock bottom" before they seek help. Perhaps this is why more people don't get treatment for their addiction. Maybe they are waiting for their "bottom" to hit.

But it's a different place for each addicted individual, what they deem unacceptable for their own life. If there's a suffering of any consequence, that's reason enough to seek help. My hopes for every addict are that they awaken to their destructive behavior(s) before they suffer unnecessary consequences to their actions and that they avoid hitting "rock bottom."

The Facts

The National Institute on Drug Abuse (2018) estimates that only about eleven percent of people with a substance abuse problem seek treatment. I also want to note that though addiction affects men and women equally, more men seek treatment than women; unfortunately for women, the stigma is greater. Be a part of the eleven percent, and we can make that percentage rise.

Writing Exercise

- ☐ *Are you experiencing out of control behavior (the kind you can't stop)?*

- ☐ *Have others suggested you should stop and ways to do so?*

- ☐ *Ever tried ways to stop, and if so, how?*

- ☐ *Are you successful and meeting goals or does your fix stand in your way?*

- ☐ *What successes did your addiction trick you into believing?*

- ☐ *Do you recognize yourself in any of the identifiers in the "beginning to your end"?*

- ☐ *Ever gotten really honest with yourself or someone else as to how bad it really is?*

- ☐ *Ever realize it's really bad but can't quit it?*

- ☐ *Anyone ever tried to intervene on your behalf?*

CHAPTER 7 –
GETTING CLEAN AND SOBER

"Your past doesn't define you, it prepares you."
- Darren Hardy

I got to treatment in 1989 on Labor Day weekend. With so many staff members gone; it looked more like a sports camp. I remember seeing people on the lawn playing Frisbee or throwing a football. I saw volleyball games and even golf clubs being swung. Suddenly I thought, "I get it! This will be great, I'll clean up for thirty days, get in shape, and go back to New York being able to handle things better." I would learn some tips on how to control drugs and alcohol in my life.

Considering I was still high and had a multitude of drugs in my system (I was still doing Quaaludes on the plane), I spent the first three days in the medical unit detoxifying. Not a pleasant experience to say the least. I remember thinking I would rather die than feel what I was going through. It was like something inside of me was trying to get out, I suppose in a sense there was; my skin was crawling as if being turned inside out. The best position was in a ball on the bed. Moving hurt every pore of my body. Shower water felt like needles being thrown at me. It was three days of hell on earth. I know they were giving me something for the pain, but I couldn't say what it was now, or that I remember it helping the pain at all. But, after the physical cravings died down, at about the three-day mark, I started to feel better or at least somewhat human again.

I learned a lot in those thirty days. I came to understand that addiction had quite a few requirements of me, and because of them, I was in the predicament I was in. It became clear this wasn't a facility that was going to teach me how to keep my using in control, but rather, they were suggesting I shouldn't use at all. Complete abstinence.

I was told that because of the length of time I had been using, thirty days was most likely not going to be enough time under my belt to stay clean and sober. It was recommended I stay another four months in a sober house.

I learned that I was given two ears and one mouth so I could listen twice as much as I talked.

And, so, I decided to stop all my talking and listen. If my best thinking had gotten me here, maybe it was time to listen to others for a change. And so I did.

I went to the sober house for four months. I also quit my job on Wall Street and became a dishwasher (literally, there was no dishwashing machine) at the Day By Day Café in St. Paul, Minnesota, a place where sober folks were given a new start. It was one of my biggest lessons in humility to date.

Humility is one of the ingredients to staying sober I will talk about later. It's not thinking less of yourself; it's thinking about yourself less. Losing the grandiose posture, understanding we all are fallible, and coming to terms with our imperfections are parts of that humility. Addicts tend to overcompensate with ego what we lack in integrity and self worth. Humility tames the ego, keeps it in check.

I met with counselors, I went to AA meetings, and I stayed sober. I thought I had made it, that I was in the clear. I was speaking monthly at the treatment center where I had once been a patient. I went into business with a friend I had met in AA, a brokerage business of a different commodity, this time precious metals. I started making good money again. I met my future wife, bought a place for us, and got married. Bought a bigger place and had two daughters. I went into business for myself, made more money, bought an even bigger house and then a second house. Life was good.

Until it wasn't.

Writing Exercise

☐ *Ever bargained with yourself on ways to control your using?*

☐ *What measures have you taken to control your fix of choice?*

☐ *What are your thoughts about stopping your fix of choice?*

☐ *What does your fix of choice protect you from?*

☐ *When have you listened to someone else that has your best interest in mind?*

CHAPTER 8 –
RELAPSE AND
CROSS-ADDICTION

"The secret of life, though, is to fall seven times and to get up eight times."
- Paulo Coelho, The Alchemist

When I met my wife, Dana, in January 1992, I made my first trip to Las Vegas to meet her father. She had spent a lot of time there, growing up over the years, and was excited to share her "spot" with me. As I explained earlier, I had started my fixation on gambling at age nine. However, once I moved over to drugs and alcohol, gambling had taken a back seat to my new fixes of choice. Though I had gotten clean and sober, I hadn't thought about (nor had anyone else) the gambling piece that had been tucked away.

I bought lottery tickets here and there, I bet on the golf course in the summer or cards in the clubhouse in the winter, I bet on sports occasionally, but I had never spent time in a casino. When I went to Las Vegas for that first time, I had no reason to believe there might be a problem with the situation.

I didn't notice a high from the gambling like I had from drugs, I didn't notice the urge to binge like I had with drugs, I didn't notice the lack of interest for anything other than the casino games like I had with drugs, but in hindsight it was all there. I was just too caught up in the euphoria of gambling to notice. It was the perfect cross-addiction for a drug addict like me.

Addicts easily slide from one addiction to the next; I had crossed over that weekend.

I came back from Las Vegas and immediately started talking about when we could go next. It became another obsession, my new fix of choice. In between trips, I found my way to the casino on an Indian reservation just twenty minutes from my backyard. Between Las Vegas and the Indian reservation casinos, the sports betting, and whatever else I could throw money at, I was gambling on a daily basis. (Rules of Addiction #8. Addiction requires too much space in your brain.)

The Vegas trips happened monthly. It wasn't long until I became Bally's number one slot player and along with it came all the perks extended to the high rollers. We were flown in, given penthouses the size of a large home, loaded with anything our hearts desired, including a butler on call 24/7. We frequented with the kids and the nanny, enticed by shopping sprees, show tickets, concert tickets, fight tickets, and limo rides for anything the kids or we might like to attend.

Again, my false impression of success and having "made it." (Rules of Addiction #11. Addiction makes you delusional.)

My gambling at home escalated also. I got in with the "big boys" on the golf course. We would make these crazy weekend trips to northern Minnesota and spend three days golfing forty-five holes a day. The stakes were anywhere from $200 to $2,000 a hole. And at the end of three days, I had seen guys hand over checks for tens of thousands of dollars and, once, even the deed to a vacation property in the area. Fortunately, not only was I a good golfer, a 4 handicap, I also worked well under pressure and was an extremely clutch player. I typically came out on top of the winnings. (Rules of Addiction #10. Addiction demands you do things you wouldn't otherwise do.)

Sometime during my marriage and after I found Las Vegas—around 1997—I had knee surgery. The first surgery didn't fix the problem, and it wasn't until three surgeries later they found a cyst lodged in my ACL. By the time that surgery finally took care of the pain, I was hooked on the OxyContin they had been prescribing me. When the prescriptions ran out from the three doctors I was milking for pain pills, I turned to the black market. My habit escalated to 640 milligrams a day. For reference, after knee surgery, I was prescribed forty milligrams a day. My habit was costing me $640 a day. (Rules of Addiction #12. Your fix of choice will require you to use/do more and more over time.)

I was buying one hundred oxy's, eighty milligrams each, for $8,000 at a time from anyone who could get their hands on them. My most dependable supplier had run out—his connection, a nurse at a large hospital who would steal them, got busted and sent to prison.

Addiction is a slippery slope, and cross-addiction is something that has to be watched out for. As previously mentioned, cross-addiction will always lead back to the fix of choice; it's just a matter of time if it's not in check.

The National Institute on Drug Abuse (2018) states an addiction, just as any other chronic disease relying on treatment to maintain, always has risk of relapse. Relapse does not mean treatment failed; it means treatment needs to be modified or a new plan of treatment implemented. It means finding other ways to change deeply rooted behaviors.

But here's the problem, as with any chronic disease, recovery doesn't always have a revolving door. Going in and out may work for a time, but one of those times you go back out there, there won't be a way back in. This goes back to Rules of Addiction #13. Here, I'll remind you: untreated addiction will end in one of three ways: jails, institutions, or death. You get to choose your destiny. You either treat your addiction, or in time, your addiction will treat you to one of those three fates. You may get away with it for a long time, but I guarantee a life of agony while you do. Your addiction wants you dead, but it will settle for a lifetime of misery. Until you get into recovery, this is what you have to look forward to.

Relapsing is a preventable condition. The addict must practice total abstinence and avoid high-risk situations because the craving always has the potential of coming back; therefore, there has to be a prevention plan. This plan must be as resolute as the treatment plan. As with any other disease—heart disease, diabetes, kidney disease, or the like—relapse is inevitable if a prevention plan is not in place.

The Facts

In recent research, relapse has been defined as a series of setbacks along the way to recovery. These mistakes, or relapses, are considered part of the recovery process, and from this perspective, not a failure to recovery. Along with this, rather than relapse being a random event, it is due to an underlying process that has to be addressed. This is why the aftercare plan to treatment is essential to success in recovery.

Drug addiction statistics support how necessary aftercare is. Though relapse statistics vary depending on the addiction, they show between forty to eighty-five percent of individuals relapse and return to using within one year of treatment, and more than two-thirds of these individuals do this within just weeks to months of beginning addiction treatment.

The longer an individual can sustain abstinence, the greater the chances of long-term recovery are. It is imperative for the addict to adhere to an aftercare plan.

Let's look at the warning signs of relapse:

- Change in mood or behaviors
- Becoming intolerant, angry, or resentful
- Increased feeling of apathy
- Isolation from others
- Socially checking out
- Not going to treatment or meetings
- Adhering to an aftercare plan but not actively participating

- Not expressing emotions

- Change of eating or sleeping habits

- Lapse in taking care of oneself mentally or physically

- Not being grateful in recovery

- Being in denial

- Relaxing of self-imposed rules

- Cravings for the fix of choice

- Thinking about the people and places associated with using

- Romanticizing past using behavior rather than remembering the pain it caused

- Minimizing the consequences of the addiction

- Bargaining with yourself

- Lying to others

- Thoughts on how to better control using

- Planning a relapse or looking for opportunities to use

I keep myself in check by thinking of a balance beam scale with two sides, one side of the scale with my recovery and the other with my addiction. My goal is to keep the side of recovery higher in the balance of the two. If I am thinking and behaving in accordance to my recovery, then that side of the scale will be higher and I am doing the work I need to stay abstinent. Likewise, if my thinking and behaving are in accordance to my using, that side will be higher and I am closer to relapsing. It is a precarious balance that has to be in check—a metaphor for my life.

Here are some questions you can ask yourself to check if your life is in balance. If your focus is out of whack, I'm guessing your answers to these questions won't be ideal.

Am I putting my recovery first and taking care of myself?

How I'm doing at home? Am I cleaning up, cleaning out? How are my relationships?

How am I doing at work? Am I getting along with my co-workers, showing up on time, and meeting my goals?

How am I on the roads? Am I cutting people off, flipping people off, screaming or yelling at cars?

People in long-term recovery share the experience of serenity. Contrary to serenity, in active addiction there is only chaos bouncing between ups and downs, highs and lows. Through consistently doing the work it takes for recovery; an addict can remain calm and unflappable even in the most extraordinary of circumstances. When we are using or the warning signs creep in, our ups and downs can be volatile. For an addict, the highs are extreme and the lows are treacherous. The goal is consistency and balance.

Writing Exercise

☐ Have you stopped one addictive behavior and ended up finding a different one?

☐ What types of fixes have you crossed over to?

☐ Did it cause you to feel the same way as your original fix of choice?

☐ Did you realize it was a cross-addiction or problem for you?

☐ In what ways did it keep you delusional?

☐ What kinds of consequences did the fix(es) of choice cause in your life?

☐ Did cross-addictions lead you back to your fix of choice?

☐ Have you been a victim of relapse?

- ☐ *Did you pick up right where you left off or was it a fast progression back to that point?*

- ☐ *Do you feel the door will always revolve for you?*

- ☐ *Do you recognize any of the warning signs to relapse in yourself?*

- ☐ *Do you find yourself isolating from others, either physically or emotionally?*

- ☐ *Do you prioritize sobriety over a new fix of choice or obsession?*

- ☐ *Do you fantasize about the fix of choice?*

- ☐ *Do you minimize the consequences of your addiction?*

- ☐ *Do you spend time plotting your next fix?*

CHAPTER 9 –
CONSEQUENCES

*"You will suffer one of two pains; the pain of discipline
or the pain of regret. The pain of discipline weighs ounces.
The pain of regret weighs tons."*
- Jim Rohn

After the knee surgery, I had steered away from all the disciplines that had kept me in recovery. I had lost my connection to any type of spirituality; for that matter, I had lost my connection with my body and mind, too. Not to mention everyone who was close to me. Once again I was isolated and alone. I chose to push away anyone who cared about me that didn't validate my behavior. My wife stopped accompanying me to Las Vegas or any other casino, and I surrounded myself with people I could buy. I would pay for their trips, gambling debts, drugs, alcohol, and whatever else I needed to in order to keep up the appearance of not having completely lost my way. (Rules of Addiction #2. Your addiction dictates where you hang out and who you hang out with.)

However, things still hadn't gotten "bad enough." I would have told you at the time I was still in control. I still had a successful business, I still had the money I needed to support my habits, I still had a wife and kids, and I still had both my homes and all my material goods. (Excuse #1. If it gets really bad, I'll quit.)

Until I didn't.

I was delusional. I wasn't in control of my using; I didn't use drugs and gambling. They used me. They consumed me.

It was January 2005, and I was about to encounter severe consequences. After two years of my wife asking me, unsuccessfully, to slow down on the gambling, she asked me to move out. She said she would give me six moths to clean up my act. No drugs, no gambling, and then she would talk. She didn't care where I went; a hotel was fine with her. She just wanted me gone. I was devastated. After two years of asking without action, I guessed she was all talk.

I didn't know where to go or what to do. I had no relatives in Minnesota to take me in, and I was in no condition to ask any decent community members or friends I had once associated with. But I was determined to make it right and get my shit together.

Except I couldn't.

I was trying to resist the temptations. I call this self-willing it. The attempts we make to keep our addiction in control. It's a combination of the lies we tell ourselves, the excuses we use, and our attempts to quit or control our behavior. It's impossible.

As the saying goes, what you resist persists. Psychologist Carl Jung first stated the concept as such, "what you resist not only persists, but will grow in size." This is a quintessentially accurate way to see addiction. And I was trying with all my might to resist. It goes back to what your mind is thinking about. By constantly thinking about what I wasn't supposed to be doing, I was just making it harder to stop. Resisting isn't the answer; the answer is in surrendering and believing in something greater than yourself. Self-willing it is impossible; looking outside of self is the answer.

You see, as much effort as I put into my recovery the first time around, I hadn't found the spiritual piece of truly believing in a power greater than myself, a higher power. I talked the talk and I may have even thought I believed in a higher power, but in actuality, this was the hardest piece of recovery for me to figure out.

Alcoholics Anonymous speaks of turning your life and addiction over to a higher power. Though often interpreted as "God," truly, a higher power is anything you can philosophically believe in, outside of yourself, that you can draw strength from and that keeps you accountable. It has everything to do with spirituality, not religion. In fact, religion can be an obstacle or a conduit to spirituality. It is different for each individual. It is left up to each person to define their higher power for themselves. Common beliefs of a higher power are nature, music, the universe, or humanity as a whole. It can be the sun or the moon—anything that inspires.

Maybe this will help you understand the difference. Religion is for people trying to stay out of Hell; spirituality is for people who have already been through Hell. If you're someone that has already been through bouts of Hell, you must find a power greater than yourself to believe in. Self-willing it will fail you every time; it's just a matter of time.

My six months was dwindling and I couldn't stop, any of it. I lied of course. I told Dana I had stopped gambling, but then inadvertently a statement of some sort would show up at the house. She would undoubtedly open it and see where I had been or that I'd taken money out (most often at the casino). I would even try to explain I had gone to the casino only to buy cigarettes because they were cheaper on the reservation. As if she would actually believe it. Delusion is a mad part of the disease, and like I said, I had lost all connection with my mind. (Rules of Addiction #11. Addiction makes you delusional. Rules of Addiction #13. Addiction will rob you of your body, mind, and spirit.)

In a last ditch effort to save my marriage and find abstinence from gambling, I moved in with my sponsor. I figured that would show Dana my commitment to changing. My sponsor and his wife regularly brought people into their home, immersing them in the 12-step program; I would be working with them and half a dozen others on my recovery.

Unfortunately, by the time I got there, my time was about up, and that July—six months after Dana had told me to leave—she served me with divorce papers. She thought I would handle it better while in the company of my sponsor; she was wrong. I couldn't imagine she would ever follow through with divorce, give up the lifestyle, or give up on me. In my sick mind and with a bankrupt spirit, I still thought she'd be a fool to leave me. My grandiosity had taken over once again, humility something long forgotten. (Rules of Addiction #13. Addiction will rob you of your body, mind, and spirit. Rules of Addiction #14. You will suffer severe consequences.)

The process took four bitter years because I fought it every step of the way. Two years into the process, we went to trial. It took two days, and by the end, the judge had had enough of me. I was blurry eyed and slurring at times, avoiding the questions posed to me, and rambling on about who knows what. At one point I tried to convince the judge that it was my disease of addiction that had lead to my marital problems and I shouldn't be held responsible to Dana in the divorce. In justification of that, I told him controlling the disease of addiction is like trying to control diarrhea, you just can't stop it. I was dead serious, but everyone else in the room, including the judge, found it rather humorous. Late in the afternoon on Friday, the second day of the trial, the judge said to me, "Mr. Marion, I am leaving at four o'clock to go hunting with my son. I would appreciate it if you could just answer the questions, so we can all be done with this by then."

Ninety days later, the judge handed down our divorce decree. Dana was awarded full physical custody of our two daughters and both our homes to include the homestead in Excelsior, Minnesota and our vacation home in Prescott, Arizona. I was to pay her (in round numbers) $28,000 a month for life. Once again, I was devastated; even she was shocked. She was awarded more than she had ever asked for. (Rules of Addiction #14. You will suffer severe consequences.)

I fired my attorney and hired an appeals attorney to appeal my case to the state court. In the end, I didn't appeal, but it took an additional two years of negotiations between attorneys to settle the financial component of our divorce and finally put it behind me. We had spent a half a million dollars on attorney fees between the two of us, and she got most everything anyway, proving I was in complete denial of my addictions and the consequences they would have. (Rules of Addiction #11. Addiction makes you delusional. Rules of Addiction #14. You will suffer severe consequences.)

I moved into a penthouse apartment at a premier, swanky, up-scale complex outside of Downtown Minneapolis overlooking Lake Calhoun. Having lost most everything, and with no one looking over my shoulder, my addictions to both drugs and gambling continued to escalate. (Rules of Addition # 12. Your fix of choice will require you to use/do more and more over time.)

I woke up one morning in 2008, having taken my last OxyContin around nine p.m. the previous night, and realized I was out. At about the twelve-hour mark, without a fix, I knew I was in trouble. I was already in so much pain from the withdrawals; I was desperate. I called a friend, also an addict of OxyContin, and asked if he had some to hold me over. He told me he couldn't get any either, but said he'd figure out something to help me. It was about an hour later when he came over, put out a line of white powder, handed me a rolled up bill and said, "Here, snort this." When I asked, "What is it?" he simply responded, "Don't ask; just snort it." And with that I did my first line of heroin and had a new fix of choice. (Rules of Addiction #10. Addiction demands you do things you wouldn't otherwise do.)

I was part of the opioid epidemic and now a heroin addict.

With my addictions running rampant, I started using company funds to feed them. I was taking my clients' money and gambling it away rather than buying the product they had paid for. I was delusional, once again, thinking I would somehow win the money back. The gambling just perpetuated itself as the need to make the money back increased. My addiction told me if I was losing at the machines, I should stay because my luck was about to turn, and if I was winning I should stay because I was on a roll. It's a sickening disease of the mind. The head games are relentless. (Rules of Addiction #2. Your addiction dictates where you hang out and who you hang out with.)

My wife used to tell me my mind was a terrible place to go alone; I never told her how right she was. An addict's mind can be a vicious trap of unrelenting obsessive thoughts. (Rules of Addiction #8. Addiction requires too much space in your brain.)

Things at the office were getting tense. My secretary, who ran the books, had grave concerns for the company's well being. We were behind approximately $400,000 in shipping and had no money to buy product. It had all been spent on my bad habits. (Rules of Addiction #6. Addiction is a selfish disease.)

Along with the strained financial situation, there were rumors flying that the Feds were cracking down on the precious metals industry in Minnesota. The buzz in the industry was several local firms were being looked into for exactly what was going on at my company, deceptive sales practices. And, though it had never been my intention to deceive anyone, it starts to look that way to the authorities when customers are buying and a company's not delivering. (Rules of Addiction #10. Addiction demands you do things you wouldn't otherwise do.)

With so much pressure coming down on me, I knew I had to stop using. It was time, once again, to go to treatment. In December of 2010, I checked myself into a hospital for thirty days, a place where I could detox and get clean. I thought at the time this must be my bottom. It wasn't. (Rules of Addiction #15. Addiction left untreated, has one of three outcomes: jails, institutions, or death.)

Detoxing, once again, was Hell. It was everything I had remembered from the first time and so much worse. I had heard stories about detoxing from opioids and heroin, the excruciating pain from the withdrawals is one of the things that keeps an addict from quitting, but nothing could have prepared me. (Rules of Addiction #14. You will suffer severe consequences.)

I had experienced times when I didn't get a fix soon enough or didn't have the means to take the dose my body had adjusted to and felt the pain of withdrawal. But, to mentally and physically go through the body completely withdrawing off these drugs is something out of a horror movie. My mind and body contorted in ways that were pure torture.

But I did it. I got through it. And I stayed the thirty days and started the comeback of body, mind, and spirit.

My daughters became my cheerleaders. I didn't let them see me for the first week, but after that, they wanted to visit as much as they could—something they hadn't wanted to do for a very long time. It was the first time I could remember them being proud of anything I had done in years.

I got back home and back to the office with a clearer head and a new will to get my life and my business back on track. I needed help, however, and the only person that could do that was my ex, Dana. She had previously run the company, that was, until I fired her when she filed for divorce. My secretary at the time, in 2005, took over her position but didn't know how to handle the company or me.

She was afraid, in way over her head, and didn't know what to do anymore. She was no longer buying my reassurances that I would make the money back on my next big run at the casino. And, yes, you read that right, I was still gambling. I had gone through treatment for my opioid and heroin addiction but couldn't give up the gambling. Again, my delusional mind and the disease of addiction were telling me what I wanted to hear, that it wasn't that bad. Rules of Addiction #11. Addiction makes you delusional. Excuse #1. If it gets really bad I'll quit.)

My secretary suggested Dana step back in.

It was spring of 2011, and at that point, Dana and I determined the only thing to do was file for Chapter 13 bankruptcy in an effort to reorganize the company and its debt. Just as that was about to happen, the FBI, United States Postal Service, and the IRS raided my office. They took everything, all my files, computers, and anything lying around; the only thing they didn't take that day was me. That would come later.

At the time, I was living with my twenty-four-year-old girlfriend, in my penthouse apartment. At the advice of Dana, with no company to go to, no money coming in, and the chance of an indictment, I moved into the basement of our marital home. I also let go of my girlfriend whom I had kept in the dark about my addictions and the trouble I was in. I had successfully kept it all a secret from her—the extreme drug use, the excessive gambling, the finances, and how bad it really was. (Rules of Addiction #1. Your addiction requires you to use the stuff whether it's killing you or those around you. Rules of Addiction #6. Addiction is a selfish disease.)

There's an adage in AA that says you're only as sick as your secrets. I was a living example of being as sick as my secrets. Think about that, a lot. When you're keeping secrets, it keeps you stuck and sick in your disease. If you're doing things that need to be hidden, you shouldn't be doing them. If you're lying about where you are, you shouldn't be there. I used to ask my family and employees to lie for me all the time. If so and so calls, don't tell them I'm at the casino. If so and so comes by, tell them I'm out to lunch. If I don't make it to the event, tell them I'm not feeling well. It goes on and on. My secrets kept me sick for years. (Rules of Addiction #10. demands you do things you wouldn't otherwise do.)

A one-year investigation ensued as I waited on pins and needles to learn my fate. In 2012, the indictment was handed down from the Grand Jury. They felt there was enough evidence to convict me. (Rules of Addiction #14. You will suffer severe consequences.)

I'd like to point out here that my attorney arranged what they call a soft arrest. That meant when the time came I would go with my attorney and turn myself in, they wouldn't just show up unannounced somewhere and arrest me. But they were watching me, and I knew it. And with all this hanging over my head, I still couldn't stop myself from going to the casino and continuing my gambling. My addiction had that strong a noose around my neck. And because of it, the feds showed up and did exactly what I was told they wouldn't do; I was arrested, handcuffed, and thrown in the back of a police car all because I couldn't stop gambling. (Rules of Addiction #3 You cannot control it once you start.)

I was offered a two-year deal. Let me clarify: that's two years in federal prison. I said no way; I would go to trial and take my chances there. Once again, I was sure I was invincible and a trial would prove I was innocent of intent to defraud (intent meaning the resolve or determination to commit the acts I had). I never intended to hurt anyone financially; it was a direct result of my addiction. And since addiction is a disease, I honestly thought they wouldn't convict me. Once again, I was delusional. You'd think I'd have learned from my first experience at trial that the best deal is the one first offered. (Rules of Addiction #11. Addiction makes you delusional.)

At trial, the judge gave me two five-year sentences to run congruently, one for wire fraud and one for money laundering. And I was ordered to pay 3 million dollars in restitution, the amount I owed my clients. I was devastated all over again. (Rules of Addiction #14. You will suffer severe consequences.)

I had suffered the consequences of losing my wife, my kids, my company, my financial stability, and my freedom all due to the effects of my addictions. I was spiritually, emotionally, and financially bankrupt, and I was one of the lucky ones. My bottom wasn't six feet underground; it was prison. I hope for you, your bottom isn't nearly as far down as mine was.

When relapse occurs, the addiction starts right where it left off. You don't get to start over and work your way up to the problematic behaviors. No, it starts as if you had never stopped. Because of the progression of addiction, you don't stand a chance having any control over it. It's the revolving door syndrome; you never know if you have another recovery in you once you go back out. For me, I'm not willing to take that chance again. I've seen enough places I never wanted to. I don't care to see six feet under, too.

I'd like to tell you about my friend Harlan. His last relapse didn't have a revolving door.

I met Harlan when I was going to school in Tampa; we lived in the same apartment complex. We became fast friends when we discovered our common love for drugs, women, and trouble. Years later, after I had been to treatment and moved to Minnesota, I got a call from his parents begging me to save him from his drug use. He had turned his penthouse apartment at the Jockey Club in Miami into a crack house, and his parents knew it was only a matter of time before he killed himself.

I went to Miami with a sober friend for back up, and we basically kidnapped Harlan. We put him on the plane with us and took him back to Minnesota. He lived in our house of five sober guys, we took him to meetings regularly and we kept him sober. Until one day when he disappeared, and we found him smoking crack after searching crack houses in the area.

Once again we brought him home and got him sober, we even handcuffed him to the dining room table at times when we had to leave him alone. But eventually he got it. He also got married, had two boys, and opened a precious metals brokerage firm in Minneapolis where I was once an employee.

On April 1, 2000 Harlan didn't show up for work, and Harlan always showed up for work. I had a bad feeling.

I took one of the other employees, and we went to his house. We found all the doors locked and no one stirring. After exhausting all other means, I broke a window and shoved my much smaller co-worker through it. From there he opened the back door to let me in and, walking through the house, I found Harlan dead in a reclining chair in the living room.

Toxicology showed he died of a heroin overdose. Harlan had been sober four years and had never done heroin until the night he died. It was said that he snorted it, just like he would have had it been cocaine, not knowing that amount could be deadly. His revolving door didn't let him back in.

Every relapse can be likened to playing Russian Roulette. There's no doubt eventually the bullet will find you. Relapse can be prevented with an aftercare plan in place and paying attention to the warning signs I'm going to share with you.

The Facts

The depth of consequences of addiction are staggering. According to Didenko and Pankratz (2007, 9-10), two-thirds of homeless people report that drugs and/or alcohol were a major reason for their becoming homeless.

It's been reported that eighty-five percent of child abuse and neglect cases are caused by substance abuse (National Center on Child Abuse Prevention Research, 2001).

According to Forbes, drug addiction can eat up fifty percent of an addict's income and 48.3 percent of marriages involving an addict end in divorce. Or how about this statistic, for every liter of alcohol consumed annually, there is a twenty percent increase in the likelihood of divorce.

The consequences and their severity differ from addict to addict. The list of possibilities is endless. From financial issues, legal issues, family issues, mental health issues, and physical health issues to the end fates of jails, institutions, or death, addiction will reap its rewards at a cost to you. It's just a matter of how much you are willing to pay with your body, mind, spirit, or wallet.

Writing Exercise

☐ *What consequences have you suffered from your fix(es) of choice?*

☐ *In what ways have you tried to "self-will" it?*

☐ *Do you believe in a higher power, something greater than yourself?*

☐ *What lies have you told yourself and others to keep your secrets?*

☐ *To what places that you never thought you'd see has your addiction lead you?*

☐ *What means have you gone through to try to stop, if any?*

☐ *Did you pick up right where you left off or was it a fast progression back to that point?*

☐ *How many times have you been through the revolving door?*

☐ *How many more times are you willing to risk?*

☐ *Do you comprehend what your consequences will ultimately be if you don't get your addictions in check?*

CHAPTER 10 –
THE ELEVATOR ANALOGY

"Life is like an elevator.
Up or down, just make sure you get off on the right floor."
- Keith Douglas

I think of addiction and recovery as an elevator. I'm going to share this analogy and philosophy with you in hopes that it will simplify this whole process.

It goes like this. All the decisions and choices we make regarding our addiction are either taking us up (towards success, recovery) or down (towards failure, addiction) on the elevator. We all start on the first floor, meaning we all have an equal chance of success or failure. Think of the first floor as the baseline. At the top of the elevator is the penthouse floor. When you get off here, you'll find floor to ceiling windows with a magnificent view of a life full of successes. At the bottom of the elevator is the six feet underground floor. When you get off here, you've met death; recovery is no longer an option.

Every decision we make takes us closer to the penthouse or six feet under. That's not to say we can't make wrong decisions or have failures; it's inevitable and a part of the process. That's why it's an elevator; we can always get back in and change the floor we are on.

Addicts tend to live on the basement level, just one floor below the first floor. Once we get off at this floor, it's easy to get stuck here. There are no windows, and often we see no way out because the rules of addiction keep us trapped. If we continue to live in the basement, our only options are to go down in the elevator where we find the floors of institutions, then jail, and the bottom floor—six feet under.

But fortunately, on the basement level there is a rear door marked "R." If you just turn around, you'll find it; it's called recovery. Recovery allows you to get back in the elevator and ride it all the way to the penthouse floor. It's up to you what floor you will get out on; your decisions and choices will direct that for you.

The next chapters are intended to show you how to find that rear door into recovery so it becomes your choice on which floor you will reside and not your addiction's choice. My hope is your elevator will take you all the way to the penthouse.

CHAPTER 11 -
ACTION #1: WAKE UP AND PULL YOUR HEAD OUT OF YOUR ASS

"This is not a dress rehearsal; this is your life."
- Bill Murray

When you have used at least three of the excuses I referred to earlier, when you can identify with at least three of the Rules of Addiction playing out in your life, when everyone who cares about you is telling you that you have a problem, wake up; it's a problem.

If you think it's everyone else that has the issues, if you think they have it all wrong and you're the only one in your world that's right, if you think everyone else has blown it out of proportion, wake up; it's a problem.

If you have suffered consequences because of your fix of choice, if you have trouble following through with your responsibilities or obligations, if you spend an excessive amount of time thinking on or planning out your next fix, wake up; it's a problem.

If you feel depressed or anxious when you are without your fix of choice, if you have physical or emotional symptoms of withdrawal when you are without your fix of choice, or you crave or have an insatiable desire for your fix of choice, wake up; it's a problem.

This is your life and you only have one shot at it. It's time to wake up to what's really going on. If you're experiencing these problems, there might be an addiction going on in your life that needs to be treated.

I work with a client who didn't realize her drinking might be responsible for the consequences she is experiencing in her life, divorce, and strained relationships with her two daughters. We are working together to determine if addiction is playing out in her life.

She has become willing to look at what's really going on in her life and to take stock. At the time I am writing this, she is spending an undetermined amount of time abstaining from alcohol while dealing with her thoughts and feelings around it. She is headed to a vacation with her daughters, spending time with them, one on one, for the first time since she decided to stop drinking. We have talked through her nerves, and she is now feeling confident about getting honest with them regarding her drinking. She is a clear example of what I mean when I say it's time to wake up.

I have a simple saying; "If you want to start feeling good about yourself, stop doing the things that make you feel bad." I know that sounds easier than it actually is, but it truly is that simple. You just need to find the path that's right for you to start feeling good about yourself again. I'm living proof, and here to tell you, if you want to start feeling better, there is another way.

I will say it again; the fact that you're reading this book is a valuable sign that you need to wake up and pull your head out of your ass. Once you do and admit there's a problem, only then can you can get on with the rest of it.

Writing Exercise

- ☐ *Which Rules of Addiction are playing out in your life?*

- ☐ *What are the excuses you use to yourself and others?*

- ☐ *Can you see where you may be in denial about your addiction?*

- ☐ *What symptoms do you face when you try to stop your fix of choice?*

- ☐ *What things could you do to start feeling good about yourself?*

CHAPTER 12 –
ACTION #2: UNDERSTAND YOUR ADDICTION

"Addicts do everything in excess,
the only things we do in moderation are the 12 Steps."
- Anonymous

Everything in moderation, cliché, I know. But, addicts don't know moderation. That's precisely why we are addicts. If we could be moderate, we would. The fact is, as addicts we don't have that choice of will.

I use the likeness of a car headed downhill with no brakes; the longer it goes, the more speed it picks up, the more out of control it gets, and the harder it crashes. Out of control addiction isn't going to stop until the crash—unless you figure out a way to put the brakes on.

Addiction is a disease of mind, body, and spirit, and left out of control, will bankrupt all three aspects of life. It is paramount that you come to understand addiction as a chronic disease. The definition of chronic is: "Persisting for a long time or constantly recurring." The definition of disease being: "A disorder of structure or function." In essence, this is an adverse or negative condition, and it's not going away. But let's be clear, that does not mean it has to take over your life. With the right tools and plan, you have the power over the addiction.

Once you grasp this, you have a chance at recovery. Just quitting on your addiction isn't enough. As I say, addicts who "quit" their fix of choice are just self-willing it, all too often. They think of recovery as an endurance contest; it is not. It has to be thought of as a life change.

It's a process of surrendering. In the case of addiction, surrendering is not a weakness and is essential for long-term recovery. It is a willingness to give up the fight against the enemy, your addiction. One of my clients, Dan M., says when he stopped resisting the stigma of being an addict of crack cocaine, he was able to admit it to himself and eventually to others in his life. This was the first step in his process to recovery. Once the addict surrenders, they can accept the need for help.

I believe one of the reasons for the stigma that comes with addiction is rooted in the word "addict." From its very beginnings and understanding of addiction, the word itself has had a negative connotation. This gives a sense of having to hide who we are and what we do. We have come to learn the only safe place to admit our name in association with our addiction is in a room full of other addicts. This can cripple us in being honest and forthright in all areas of all life.

We've also been inundated with the word "anonymity," creating a stigma around having to be anonymous. What's important to understand in the way this word is meant is that it's not appropriate for us to break anyone else's anonymity; that's their business. But we individually and collectively have a voice that needs to be shared and heard.

Fortunately this is beginning to change, but how sad that the addiction epidemic had to become what it has to open doors that have been closed for decades. Finally people from the homeless to the White House are speaking out in all forms of media to be a voice in helping others and bringing this crisis to light.

Giving up the fight

"He that fights and runs away, May turn and fight another day;
But he that is in battle slain, Will never rise to fight again."
- Demosthenes 338BC

There is a battle going on between you and your addiction. It's up to you which one wins. Turn and run away, don't let it slay you.

As addicts we have perceived threats and fears in giving up our fix of choice. One of the things I heard early on in recovery is that nine out of ten times our fears never come to pass. I cannot tell you how often I have had to remind myself of this throughout my years, not only in recovery but in life.

Here is the definition you need to know about FEAR, False Evidence Appearing Real. Rarely, do the things we build up in our heads, the things we fear the most, ever come to fruition. Yet, we are paralyzed in taking the steps to address our addiction because we fear the unknown, and we fear giving up something that has become such a part of us; sometimes it can even feel as if we are giving up a lover or best friend (and, in some of our cases, we actually are).

Legendary philosopher, Lao Tzu, said this, "If you are depressed, you are living in the past. If you are anxious, you are living in the future. If you are at peace, you are living in the present." As addicts, we find it difficult to live in today. Our depression about the past and our anxiety about the future keep us living in fear. To address addiction, you must live in the present and do what you can do today.

Jack Canfield, best selling author says, "Everything you want is on the other side of fear." We hear all too often we have to "face our fears," but I promise, they are never as bad as we think they will be in the first place. Remember, it's false evidence that only appears real. There's nothing we cannot get through with the proper help to do so. That's where faith comes in (and I'm not talking about a faith in a religious context here but rather faith in yourself). The opposite of fear is faith. Once you replace your fear with faith, there's hope, and anything is possible. I will talk more about faith in Chapter 18.

You also need to come to terms with the impact your addiction has on those around you. There is no doubt that your behavior has caused harm to others, in one way or another; it can't be avoided. We are the afflicted and your family, friends, and coworkers are the affected.

I work as a Life Coach with L. D.; she was codependent to an addict. Her fiancé was taking her down a path she never thought she'd venture. As she put up with more and more unacceptable behavior over time, she had not realized how far she had veered from the main road. At the point he pulled a gun on her, in their shared home, she reached out to me for help. Coming to understand the hold an addict has on the people in their life, she realized he had taken her hostage on his downhill spiral. In getting the information she needed, she was able to end the relationship with her fiancé, and he moved out. Her bottom, because of the addict in her life, could have been six feet underground had she not made the changes she did.

Any addict in the throes of their addiction becomes a complete ass-hole; we have no regard for others. Everyone apparently knows it, too; there's a t-shirt I owned in college that said, "Instant Asshole Just Add Alcohol." We blame everyone and everything for our issues, make others feel guilty and responsible for our use and abuse, and have lost the ability for compassion or empathy.

We may try to fool our loved ones, pretend we care, say we're sorry, make false promises that we know we can't possibly keep, tell lies, and manipulate to make others believe whatever it is we're trying to get them to believe. But we, as addicts in active addictions, cannot possibly do any of these things because all we can truly think rationally about is how we're going to get our next fix. We have no respect or love for ourselves; how would we ever expect to have it for others? (Rules of Addiction #9. Addiction will strip you of self-love and respect.)

We keep ourselves in denial; we don't come to terms with the truth in our minds or actions. We can't possibly think about the damage we are causing and the people we are hurting that love and care about us. Why? It's so simple. It's too painful.

Those thoughts and feelings are riddled with guilt and shame. Let's take a second to talk about the difference in the two. New York Times Best selling author, John Bradshaw, refers to it this way, the difference between guilt and shame is this: guilt is "I made a mistake," and shame is "I am a mistake." As active addicts, we live in that shameful, hopeless persona.

Oftentimes, we are incapable of dealing with the emotions needed to handle these thoughts and feelings. We are emotionally handicapped. When an addict starts their addiction, their emotions stop growing. Therefore, our emotional intelligence is at the age we first started using. If you're an adult now, trying to have adult interactions and emotional relationships, it's not possible. Once a journey of recovery starts, emotions and feelings have to be learned from where we left off. This is part of the process and recovery offers the coping skills to work through these feelings.

Whatever negative effects our addiction may be causing in our lives or the lives of those around us, we fear giving it up will cause more pain and/or less happiness. Our addictions may be self-destructive or out of control, but wanting to avoid facing the struggles associated with recovery keeps us continuing the behavior. When you come to understand that every negative effect that comes from being in active addiction will be countered, overturned, and overcome while in recovery, your perception of getting in recovery will change. Understanding your addiction, its place, and its effects in your life are keys to becoming ready and willing for help.

Writing Exercise

☐ *What stigmas about your fix of choice keep you in hiding?*

☐ *Make a list of the things you fear about giving up your addiction.*

☐ *Make a list of the things you fear about getting in recovery.*

☐ *Looking at your list, what is so scary about each of these things?*

☐ *What is the worst-case scenario if these fears come true?*

☐ *Being realistic or rational, what are the more likely outcomes of these fears?*

CHAPTER 13

ACTION #3: FIND A SOLUTION THAT'S RIGHT FOR YOU

"I didn't choose to become an addict, but I do get to choose my recovery."
- David Marion

Know your options. Ask a room full of recovering addicts, and you may not find even two that found the same solution. This is where taking the time to talk with a professional is absolutely key. Google "treatment center" and 590 million results come up; Google "types of treatment for addiction," and there are 160 million results. If you want to get this right, you need direction in your approach to your recovery.

Your addiction will dictate the types of treatment plans available. But even among each addiction, there are many roads to successful recovery. Your financial situation, work situation, family situation, your mental and physical health, the length of time the addiction has been going on, as well as other factors will all play into making the decision that's right for you.

For some addicts, finding a 12-step meeting for the fix of choice will be sufficient as an option for recovery. As I mentioned earlier, I walked out of my first 12-step meeting of Alcoholics Anonymous and got high, but I know people who went to their first meeting and have been clean and/or sober ever since.

Dave T. spent ten years of his adult life spiraling out of control with drugs and alcohol. With no insurance, he didn't have the option of treatment but knew his addictions weren't an option anymore either. He was so miserable, depressed, and self-loathing, his goal became simple: just don't wake up. He says his misery, car crashes, broken bones, and morning after morning of regrets finally brought him to the point of willingness—the willingness to do whatever it takes to try something different. He went to AA, moved into a sober house, and spent as much time on his recovery as he had on his drinking and drugging. He's been clean and sober since that first AA meeting October of 2016.

The 12-Step program is the most well-known and commonly used method of recovery. Alcoholics Anonymous started in 1935 with its two founding members, Bill W. and Dr. Bob, in Akron, Ohio. Today, the 12-Step Program is a fellowship of millions worldwide and has grown to include groups for over one hundred types of meetings.

Though it's been around the longest, since that time, dozens of other methods to recovery have come into play. Alternative to the 12-Step approach, there are support groups finding success in recovery including secular groups, groups for women, and philosophy-based groups. There are groups that focus on abstinence by empowerment with their peers, and all with comprehensive principles and agendas to address abstinence.

For others, more intense types of treatment and professionals may be needed. Even among treatment centers, inpatient or outpatient, there are hundreds of options. Knowing what addictions are addressed as well as what methods used are essential. While many treatment centers are 12-Step-based there are plenty that are not. The 12-Step model is not a one-size-fits-all plan and does not work for everyone. There are different schools of thoughts on the treatment of addiction cravings and the means to recover physically, mentally, and spiritually from them.

Effective modalities can include holistic treatment; nutritional treatment; Evidence-Based Treatment (EBT); behavioral therapy, such as cognitive-behavioral therapy or contingency management; group or individual therapies; medicated-assisted treatments; alternative medicine therapies; and co-occurring or dual diagnosis disorder therapies, which address addiction when there is also a diagnosis of a mental health disorder. And these are just a few of the most common therapies!

I hope you can begin to understand the vast labyrinth of confusion the treatment of addiction can cause and why it is imperative to have someone on your side to navigate through it. In a recent New York Times blog titled "Effective Addiction Treatment," by Jane E. Brody (2013), Thomas McLellan, co-founder of the Treatment Research Institute in Philadelphia, said this, "There are exceptions, but of the many thousands of treatment programs out there, most use exactly the same kind of treatment you would have received in 1950, not modern scientific approaches."

This being the case, it's important to know what is working and what is not. Multiple stints in treatment facilities are not the answer. I'm currently working as a sober coach with Bob D.; he has been to treatment sixteen times and has spent 1.5 million dollars in those endeavors. His story is one that motivates me to write this book. Numbers like that are unacceptable.

The Brody (2013) blog goes on to say, "Often, low-cost, publicly funded clinics have better-qualified therapists and better outcomes than the high-end residential centers typically used by celebrities like Britney Spears and Lindsay Lohan."

With that being said, keep this in mind; the more a treatment facility costs does not denote the level of success one will have in recovery. The blog also states, "Contrary to the 30-day stint typical of inpatient rehab, people with serious substance abuse disorders commonly require care for months or even years, the short-term fix mentality partially explains why so many people go back to their old habits."

This is why relapse is so prevalent, and an aftercare treatment plan is critical to long-term recovery and to avoid these pitfalls. I hope you can see here how crucial it is to find the solution that is right for you, hopefully the first time and not the sixteenth like Bob.

Writing Exercise

☐ *Do you know the types of programs available to address your addiction?*

☐ *Have you tried treatments before, and if so, what kinds?*

☐ *Have you considered you may need a long-term treatment plan?*

☐ *Make a list of the issues you may need to address in order to find the right treatment plan (family, job, finances, etc).*

CHAPTER 14 -
ACTION #4: DO THE WORK

"People need to be reminded more often than they need to be instructed."
– Samuel Johnson

Wherever your solution takes you, listen to the people there. You have clearly not had your best interest in mind. They do. They are experts in their field, and they know how to take care of you.

As addicts, many of us are used to breaking the rules, not conforming to society's expectations and not listening to authorities. These are the grandiose and selfish ways about us. Drop that shit at the door. It will not serve you as you enter a place for recovery. This is where you will learn humility, and it starts now.

You are going to be thrown into all kinds of conversations, activities, and situations you are not going to like, and that will be uncomfortable for you. Remember this; there is no comfort in growth and no growth in comfort.

You are going to be put out of your comfort zone, as Darren Hardy, Success Mentor, says, "Life begins outside the edge of your comfort zone," so get okay with it. Get comfortable being uncomfortable. Your addiction has surely brought you to some uncomfortable situations; the difference here is now it's constructive and not destructive. If you could handle it in your addiction, you can handle it in your recovery.

You will be challenged emotionally, philosophically, spiritually, and possibly physically, depending on your addiction. You will be expected to talk, write, process, and engage; you will be tested to your core. It will most likely be confrontational and demanding of you. You will be dealing with thoughts, emotions, and feelings you have never considered.

Addicts use because they don't want to feel the feelings; numbing becomes a way of coping. Richard H. Siegel Ph.D. (2015) says, "Addiction is an unwillingness to be uncomfortable even as it perpetuates unwanted feelings we want to be rid of. Like a Chinese finger puzzle that only strengthens its grip when we struggle, resisting negative feelings tightens its emotional grip. The solution to the finger puzzle is to push into it, not pull away. So to be released from the grip of anger, guilt, fear, shame, sadness or rejection you can feel your feelings until they lose their grip on you."

The thing is, feelings don't last once you confront them and allow yourself to feel them. The emotional charge melts away and loses its grip on your body, mind, and spirit when given the chance to do so.

Remember when I talked about addicts having stunted their emotional growth at the age they started using? You have a lot of catching up to do, and this is the place to do it. As addicts we were born and raised but never grew up. This is where you're going to grow up in many ways. And it's a good thing; it has to happen for recovery to take place.

I had gotten an education, gone to college, and had success in my professional life, but I never learned about life. I never learned how to live in today or how to be happy, a good son, an engaged partner, or a thoughtful father until I got into recovery for my addictions.

In truth, there is no situation so dire, no challenge so great, and no choice so bewildering that it cannot be overcome. We may believe that all avenues have been closed to us or that our most conscientious efforts will not make a difference, but I promise you, there is a solution and your life can change. You just have to decide you want it. As Jim Rohn says, "Don't wish it were easier, wish you were better." You'll have to do the work.

So, be prepared to work hard and do as you're told. I'm guessing "do as you're told" might be hard for you to hear. It may remind you of a parent, spouse, teacher, or some other authority figure, but if you are sick and tired of being sick and tired of the way you've been living, get over it, and do the work. I promise you it will be worth it. There is a reason struggle comes before success (even) in the dictionary.

Writing Exercise

☐ *Are you ready to listen to others and stop thinking for yourself?*

☐ *Are you ready to grow up mentally and spiritually?*

☐ *Are you sick and tired enough of being sick and tired to do the work?*

CHAPTER 15 –
ACTION #5: AFTERCARE

"Successful people do what unsuccessful people are not willing to do."
- Jim Rohn

Putting together a long-term aftercare plan will be crucial to recovery. To avoid going back to old habits, to fend off previous instigators and triggers, and to avoid relapse, you will have to adhere to the plan put in place. A recovery professional can help you find the right ongoing solutions for you and your schedule.

At this point, you're going to have to take responsibility for yourself. I talked earlier about listening to the people who have your best interest in mind and that your thinking hadn't served you well. Adhering to your aftercare program is on you. It takes integrity, defined as this: integrity is doing what you're supposed to be doing even when no one is looking. Most likely this will be a new concept for you.

Mel Robbins, serial entrepreneur, television host, motivational speaker, and author says it like this, "Fact: You are never going to feel like it!" Do it anyway; it may just save your life.

Some of the following suggestions will be helpful.

Meetings/Support Groups

"Hang out with those who have a common future, not a common past."
- Darren Hardy

This is where I'll mention a very important statistic; according to the late Jim Rohn, author, entrepreneur, and motivational speaker, we are each an average of the five people we spend the most time with. Think about that carefully. An average of their wealth, their health, what they do and what they think about. "Choose your friends wisely" isn't just a line; it's a way of life.

As I like to say, "If you hang out in a barbershop long enough, you're going to get a haircut." And if you hang out in a bar, you'll eventually drink, in a crack house, you'll eventually smoke cocaine. If you hang out in the places and with people who validate your addiction, you're going to continue the behavior.

If you hang out with losers, you will be a loser; if you hang out with gangsters you will be a gangster; if you hang out with drug addicts, you will be a drug addict. Okay, I think I've made my point. But likewise, if you hangout with winners, you will be a winner, and if you hang out with people abstaining from an addiction, you will much more likely abstain from your addiction. If you want recovery from your *fix of choice*, you are going to have to change the places you hang out and the people you hang out with.

I'm not sure who originally said it, but I'll quote it here, "If you're the smartest person in the room, you're in the wrong room." My brother, Executive Director of an education non-profit, told me this about his success, "I'll only hire people smarter than me." The point is: don't hang out with a bunch of idiots. Surround yourself with people who have your answers, people who have gone before you and can educate and teach you. And for goodness sake, don't be judgmental. Each person you encounter is just a fellow traveler in this journey called life. You never know what your new best friend will look like. You don't know the package the person who can change your life will come in. Dr. Wayne Dyer said, "Be open to everything and attached to nothing."

Keep to your herd. Birds of a feather flock together. Find a group of other people finding success in recovery. If you were hanging out with the losers, find the winners. Go to AA, NA, SA, GA meetings, support groups, fellowship clubs, or wherever else the people of your tribe gather. Reach your hand out to meet at least three people. Listen to those that have what you lack; take what you like and leave the rest. If it resonates with you and you can implement it and use it in your life, do so. If it doesn't fit, be grateful for the suggestion and keep listening. I heard early on in meetings, "Don't speak unless you can improve upon the silence." Keep listening.

Look for the similarities in people rather than the differences. If you're looking for the differences, you will find them all day long, and with that you'll find the excuses why it won't work for you. If you look for the similarities, you'll find you have things in common and you're not terminally unique; we all have struggles, weaknesses and things to overcome, and someone will have your answers.

Make it a practice to find at least three things in common with everyone you meet. You'll start realizing everyone has something to offer and contribute; this is a way of practicing humility, and I suggest you try it.

It is important to realize that whatever your addiction, race, gender, occupation, sexual orientation, or other differentiating factors you feel set you apart, I guarantee there is a tribe in recovery for you to identify with. As it is said, your vibe will attract your tribe.

I talked about my first encounter with an Alcoholics Anonymous meeting, and I was certain no one in that room was part of my tribe. Since finding recovery, and both times I might add, I have met, and remain friends with to this day, some of the most successful, glamorous, intelligent, fun, and funny people you can imagine. People from all walks of life: politicians, attorneys, construction workers, businessmen (and women), artists, entertainers, CEO's of major corporations, stay-at-home moms, students, retirees, and everything in between. We addicts makeup an eclectic, crazy crew of folks, but when you find your herd in recovery, you'll feel like you've finally made it home. You'll learn you are not terminally unique.

Find a Mentor, Coach, Sponsor, Teacher, or Consultant

"There is no lack of knowledge out there, just a shortage of asking for help."
- Unknown

SPONSOR = Sober Person Offering Newcomer Suggestions On Recovery.

Here's a modern day parable that will help you understand the role of a sponsor.

A man was walking down a street when he fell into a hole. The walls were so steep he couldn't get out. So the man in the hole began to cry out for help.

Soon, a doctor walked by, and he heard the man's cries for help. The doctor wrote a prescription, tossed it down the hole, and walked away.

Before long, a priest walked by and heard the man calling out. "Father, can you help me?" the man asked. The priest wrote a prayer, threw it in the hole, and walked away.

Finally, a friend came along. And the man asked the friend for help.

The friend then made a brave, bold move: *He jumped into the hole.*

The man who had been trapped was aghast. "Are you stupid? Now we're both stuck down here!"

But the friend said, "Yeah, but I've been down here before, and I know the way out."

I don't care what you want to call this person in your life, but get one. There is not one person who doesn't need this kind of support, the kind from someone who has been there before. And, I don't mean just for recovery. Yes, if you're in recovery, you need someone to draw from, but think about it—there's not a successful person on the planet who hasn't had one, in any walk of life.

If you want success in recovery, it's no different than Michael Jordan wanting success at basketball, Bill Gates wanting success as an entrepreneur, or Oprah Winfrey wanting success as TV icon. You have to have coaches, teachers, mentors, consultants, or the like to get you there. Not one of those people got to where they are by self-willing it.

So, if you want to find success in recovery, get yourself a sponsor, sober coach, friend, or partner, and be accountable to them. Look for someone that has what you want and study them, pick their brain, listen to them, and emulate them. I'm not saying become a clone or change the essence of who you are. Everyone of us is as unique as our thumbprint, talented in our individual ways, and has our own special gifts, so don't make the mistake of trying to become someone you are not. But rather learn the insights, habits, mindset, and changes they have made in their lives that will get you where you want to be. Remember, we don't need a lobotomy; we just need guidance to stop our using.

Be of Service To Others

"The best way to find yourself is to lose yourself in the service of others."
- Mahatma Gandhi

Help the ones who come after you. Know you have someone else's answers. Just as you didn't know who you might come across that had what you needed, said something you needed to hear, or showed you a different way, you will do the same for someone else. Be open to the opportunity to change someone else's life. You could be their difference between life and death. Sponsor someone, be a mentor, and share your experience, strength, and hope. Welcome someone that is new to recovery. If you go to meetings or support groups, go early, stay late, set up, clean up, and be of service to others. In order to keep it, you have to give it away.

In the early days of Alcoholics Anonymous, there was a discussion between the two founding members regarding not being able to save everyone from drinking; people would come to the meetings and then go out and drink some more. Discouraged, they wondered if AA just wasn't working. But what they realized is *they* were staying sober. It was in the service work. By focusing on helping others, sobriety comes much more easily.

At work and at home, ask how you can be of help. Pitch in, do what you can. Most likely you've been a burden to those around you, so try making up for it by putting others first. For me, the more I make my life about others, the better I get to feel. What you give is what you get. When I was using, I didn't care about anything or anyone else. In recovery, I take pride in redeeming myself.

Journaling

"Your Journal is like your best friend, You don't have to pretend with it, you can be honest and write exactly how you feel."
- Bukola Ogunwale

Journaling is way to express your feelings, track your progress, and share your insights with yourself. It can be encouragement, inspiration, or comfort. It's a perfect place to contemplate who your are, what you want, and your purpose. Each and every one of us has unique and special talents; in order to find out our purpose, we must figure out our gifts.

You can explore these ideas and list goals and your accomplishments towards them. It is a way to be mindful of your thoughts and behaviors and to make sure you're on track with your commitments to yourself. Journaling is also a safe place for your emotions to come out and be explored.

Psychology Today reports that studies show journaling to be healing emotionally, physically, and psychologically. It's also an emotional release that lowers anxiety and stress and induces better sleep. Young adults assigned to keep a gratitude journal, chronicling things they were grateful for, showed greater increase in determination, attention, enthusiasm, and energy compared to other groups.

Journaling, in essence, can be a powerful component of long term care in recovery. I've seen some of the greatest miracles take place when pen is put to paper. And, who knows, it may even inspire you to write a book someday.

Therapies, Medications, and Nutrition

"An over-indulgence of anything,
even something as pure as water, can intoxicate."
- Criss Jami

It's important to keep up with any type of recommended therapies, medications and nutrition. If you work with a psychiatrist, psychologist, an LADC (Licensed Alcohol and Drug Counselor), addictionologist, addiction nutritionist, or other professional, you will want to keep up on your appointments and commitment to your therapy.

The connection between addiction and psychiatric disorders is not uncommon; fifty percent of all addicts suffer from a serious mental illness that needs to be addressed. Professionals can help with dual diagnoses, also known as co-occurrence issues. In fact, there are now co-occurrence specialists working in this newer field of study. Because these two diagnoses can feed each other, as mental illness is often a cause of addiction, both need to be treated aggressively.

It's imperative to get to the bottom of your addiction and dig it out by the tangled roots of yesterday so you can live unencumbered in today. When you understand how and why your addiction has manifested, along with the proper treatment, the journey of recovery can begin.

It is likely that when mental illness exists, medications can help. Antidepressants, anti-anxiety medications, and mood stabilizers can be extremely effective, especially short term. Ultimately, it is always the goal to recondition the brain (chapters 18-20) and the gut brain (chapter 21) so that no medication is needed at all. But when mental illness is part of the equation, it is most important to listen to the medical professionals.

In the case of opioids, heroin, and other chemical dependency addictions, a regiment of methadone or Suboxone may be an option. These medications satisfy the dependent person's need for the drug, suppress the withdrawal symptoms and cravings, and can be essential in detoxifying an addict from their drug of choice. However, these practices need to be short-term solutions, with the ultimate objective to be free of any substance.

Victoria Abel, Addiction Nutritionist to treatment centers throughout Arizona, says the goal with these therapies is five to seven days. That's it. She says, "If you're going to be sober, let's be sober." Victoria's field of expertise, using the approach of nutrition, is one of the fastest growing areas in psychiatry and in treating addiction. This field of work concentrates on healing the body by giving it the proper nutrition it is lacking responsible for the cravings in the addict.

When I met Josh H., he had been on Suboxone for ten years. When we first discussed his getting off the Suboxone, his reaction was that of a typical addict at the thought of giving up his fix of choice. This is a problem; it's simply a shift in addictions and not a solution.

Victoria says, "These people are just walking around high and recovery can't possibly begin," Harm reduction programs such as methadone and Suboxone are a necessity at times in detoxing, but healing the body is the answer, not more drugs. In too many cases, the addict becomes as dependent on them as they did their fix of choice.

These areas of aftercare are just some of the ways in which recovery takes place. Advisors, as well as professionals, along with the addict, need to work together in finding the appropriate solution to recovery for each individual.

Writing Exercise

- ☐ *What things do you put off because you don't feel like doing them?"*

- ☐ *How's your level of integrity?, Do you do what you're supposed to when no one is watching?*

- ☐ *How are the five people you hang out with the most doing in their lives?*

- ☐ *Are you open to change or attached to everything as you know it?*

- ☐ *Where has your best thinking gotten you at this point?*

- ☐ *What mentors, teachers, or coaches do you have advising you?*

- ☐ *What are the people who have your best interest in mind telling you?*

- ☐ *In what ways does your addiction make you selfish?*

- ☐ *In what ways can you be of service to others?*

- ☐ *What aftercare methods can you see as beneficial in your life?*

CHAPTER 16

A NEW DIRECTION

"The path from dreams to success does exist. May you have the vision to find it, the courage to get on to it, and the perseverance to follow it."
- ***Kalpana Chawla***

In Earl Nightingale's, *"The Strangest Secret"* (1950 radio show available on YouTube), he talks of the consequences of not having a direction in life. He likens it to a ship in the harbor without a navigation plan. There may be a whole crew onboard, captain and all, but without a plan in direction, the ship will bounce around the harbor, get tossed and turned about, and most likely never make it out to sea. Addiction is the same.

I know when I was actively using my fixes of choice, I had no direction, bounced around, got tossed and turned, and never made it anywhere other than prison. I'm guessing you can relate. It's like this: it's hard to get to where you're going if you don't have a plan from where you're at.

Coming up with a plan is fundamental for a new life in recovery. Part of that plan needs to include new disciplines to change the errors of the past. "To arrive in a well-designed place, you need a well-designed plan," says Jim Rohn. You will arrive, but where? It's your choice of what that destination looks like.

Think of where you are right now. You have arrived. Whether by your design or the fact you didn't have a design, it is where you are. Where do you want to arrive in your future? You cannot change the destination overnight, but you can change the direction, and a new direction will determine the destination. It's small, consistent changes in direction that will impact your journey to arrive where you want to be.

Be disciplined in this new direction. I will repeat Jim Rohn's quote from Chapter 9 because it's that important. "You will suffer one of two pains; the pain of discipline or the pain of regret. The pain of discipline weighs ounces. The pain of regret weighs tons." The stakes of regret for an addict are way too high.

I don't think it's a coincidence that you are reading this book; I suggest it's your destination. Your journey has led you here. You can change your life, or you can give this book to someone else that may find it valuable. It's a matter of where you want your destiny to end.

Writing Exercise

☐ *Where have you arrived; what's your life look like right now?*

☐ *Was this by your design or by happenstance?*

☐ *What small changes can you make in your direction?*

CHAPTER 17 –
TURNING YOUR LIFE AROUND

"The chains of habit are too weak to be felt
until they are too strong to be broken."
- Samuel Johnson

Your addiction either controls you or you control it. You decide which way it's going to be. I promise you, you are stronger than your addiction. You just have to believe it, too. Stop telling yourself you'll never get it, you're too overwhelmed, it's too much to change, you can't do it, recovery is for other people but not you, that you're too far gone, the habit is too bad, it's too hard to break, blah, blah, blah. I've not only heard it all before; I've felt it all before. This is the part where you have to change your mind. You're only as weak as your thoughts. And therefore it is essential to change your thoughts.

I sponsor a guy who at one time or another said all these things. He had chronically relapsed since he was fifteen years old. He admitted to me he hadn't been sober for more than three months at a time since then—he is now fifty. At the time I'm writing this, he has been clean and sober for nine months and counting, has moved back in with his wife who had previously kicked him out, and enjoys his young children who had been afraid to be left alone with him when he was using. These are the miracles that I am privileged to see frequently when the beliefs about oneself change.

This is the part of book where I'm going to get a little spiritual and philosophical on you. This piece is going to make a huge impact on your recovery once you figure it out. It was the last component I put together, the piece I struggled with the most, and the part I hadn't gotten the first time I entered into recovery.

Remember the part about how you'll become what your thoughts attend to? This is where all those phrases you have heard come into play: act as if, fake it till you make, as a man thinketh, where attention goes energy flows, thoughts become things, etc, etc, etc. Change your thoughts; change your life (actually the title of a book by Dr. Wayne Dyer), and it's absolutely true.

Thinking positive is a way of life that has to be adopted. Positive thoughts bring about positive results. The glass is half full versus half empty. You have to starve out the negative. When the negative thoughts, such as the ones above, come across your brain, you have got to get rid of them. I like to say negative people have a problem for every solution. Don't be that person.

Andy Dooley, entrepreneur and motivational speaker, encourages saying this when negative thoughts creep in, "Stop, cancel, clear, get the fuck (or fear) out of here." Try that on. You have to replace those thoughts immediately with positive affirmations such as, I'm getting better every day; I am working towards changing my life; if those that have gone before me can, I can too; I am stronger than my addiction; etc, etc, etc.

Have you heard the tale of "Two Wolves"? In case you have, here it is again. If you have not, it is very profound and pertinent to your life.

One evening an old Cherokee Indian told his grandson about a battle that goes on inside people. He said, 'My son, the battle is between two 'wolves' inside us all. One is Evil. It is anger, envy, jealousy, sorrow, regret, greed, arrogance, self-pity, guilt, resentment, inferiority, lies, false pride, superiority, and ego.

The other is good. It is joy, peace, love, hope, serenity, humility, kindness, benevolence, empathy, generosity, truth, compassion, and faith.'

The grandson thought about it for a minute and then asked his grandfather: 'Which wolf wins?'

The old Cherokee simply replied, 'The one you feed.'

I am here to tell you, be careful of which wolf you feed. Our thoughts can be our worst enemy.

For decades it was a popular belief that it took twenty-one days to form a new habit. However, more recently, Phillippa Lally, a health psychology researcher at University College London, published a study in the *European Journal of Social Psychology*. Lally and her research team decided to figure out just how long it actually takes to form a habit. It was concluded that on average it took sixty-six days.

She also found how long it takes can vary widely depending on the behavior, the person, and the circumstances. Have realistic expectations when it comes to changing your habits; the study showed it can take anywhere from two to eight months for a new habit to form. Do these positive affirmations whenever negativity arises, and in time, your brain will form the habit of thinking positive.

We also need to talk about having an "attitude of gratitude." I'm sure you've heard this one before, too. This is another game changer. Stop focusing on how bad it is, what you don't have, what you've lost, etc. and start focusing on what you have to be grateful for. It can be as minimal as the sun shining or the rain coming down, the hair on your head or the shoes on your feet; nothing is too insignificant to appreciate. Here's something for you to think about. When I heard it, it turned my thinking 180 degrees; *I thought I needed new shoes until I saw a man with no feet.*

I'll share with you an experience I had while I was incarcerated to reiterate the point. Locked up in federal prison, it was the day of my daughter's high school graduation. That made it one of the more difficult days to get through. One of the days where all I could do was kick myself for my transgressions. Life was going on without me, milestones were being made, and I all I could do was climb the walls, literally and figuratively, mentally and physically because I was missing it all.

I went to the chapel that day where I saw an inmate that had been down for eighteen years. When he saw me, he couldn't help but notice my normally cheerful and positive demeanor had been erased. He asked me why so. I told him the reason for my sad state of being, missing my daughter's graduation. He gave me a whole new perspective and a turning point in my recovery.

Since the time he had been locked up his mother had passed away, his daughter had overdosed, and his son had been murdered. His only look into what was going on in his family's life on the outside was through videos of the funerals on the inside of the prison's chapel.

We have to count our blessings. We have to be grateful. As bad as it may get, you don't have to look far to find someone who has it worse. This practice will retrain your brain. By focusing on what's good, the positive, and not dwelling on the bad, the negative, more good will come into your life. Find things, anything, to be grateful for. It is a scientific fact, written about by Alex Korb in *Psychology Today* (2012), that people who come from a gratitude mindset are happier, healthier, and live longer.

All too often the belief is "I will be happy when _____" (just fill in the blank). The problem with this line of thinking is, it absolutely, one hundred percent, won't ever work. It's actually the exact opposite. If you want happiness to find you, you have to "act as if" it is already so. Think about this: you do not need anything more, at any given moment in time, to be happy. You can choose happiness. I used to say when I'm successful, I'll be happy; today I say, if I'm happy, I'm successful. Remind yourself of that often.

These schools of thought fall under the Universal Law of Attraction and it is one of the Twelve Universal Laws that govern our universe. The Law of Attraction dictates how we create the things, events, and people who come into our lives. Our thoughts, feelings, words, and actions produce energies, which in turn, attract like energies. Negative energies attract negative energies, and positive energies attract positive energies.

You need to know and understand the Law of Attraction is playing out and working in your life at all times. Using it to your advantage can turn your addiction around and improve upon your health, wealth, and personal relationships.

Let me ask you this, have you ever had something really good happen to you and thought "this is too good to be true"? And then when it turned out to be "too good to be true" you said, "I knew it was too good to be true." Why do you think that happened? I'll tell you why. It wasn't that it was too good to be true; it was that you thought it was too good to be true.

Or ever thought something good was coming your way but thought, "I'm not going to tell anyone" or "I'm not going to count on it" because you thought you'd jinx it? Well, guess what, at that thought, you jinxed it. You obviously didn't really believe it, otherwise you would have shouted it from the rooftops as if it had already happened. Maybe you've heard of it this way: a self-fulfilling prophecy. Call it what you will; what you're thinking, you are manifesting.

This is your subconscious brain sabotaging you, and it has to be retrained. Your subconscious controls ninety-five percent of your life. That means with your conscious mind, you will only get five percent of your desired results as you try to have control over your life. This is why "self-willing it" does not work. Self-willing it is trying to change your life by using your conscious brain, when in actuality it's the subconscious brain that needs to be changed.

Forming a new habit is the way to retrain the subconscious brain. I heard it explained like this: think of a habit as highway that you use every-day to get back and forth to work. The drive becomes a habit when your subconscious brain takes over, and you don't even have to think any longer about the route itself; it just becomes automatic.

If the highway were to close and you would have to find a new road to get to work, you would start to create a new habit. You may head to the old highway now and again when you're not paying attention, but eventually you won't. Remember, we talked about a new habit taking two to eight months of consistent attention? After that amount of time, when the new route to work becomes automatic, you have retrained the subconscious; it's a new habit.

The old highway may still be used by some trespassers or people taking walks, but eventually, without maintenance, it will start to crack and decay. The weeds will start taking over, and finally it will become unrecognizable for use; that habit is gone.

This is how to forge new habits. When you do this, you will attract the life of your design. You decide what you put into your subconscious, focus on that, and bring into existence the life you want to start living.

And before I get off the subject, let me add one more thing. Your subconscious is like a recorder that's on 24/7. It hears everything, including your thoughts at all times, and programs it. Whether you are sleeping or awake, feed it only the good stuff.

Before it was first published in 1877 as *The Law of Attraction*, by Russian author and philosopher Helena Blavatsky, the belief was called the *New Thought Movement* based on the teachings of Phineas Quimby in the early 19th century. Early in his life, Quimby was diagnosed with tuberculosis, and when medical treatments weren't working, he set his mind to curing himself. He found when he was excited by things such as galloping on his horse, the pain subsided, and so he set on his path to healing his body with his mind. (Perhaps you've heard "mind over matter." The same principle applies.) These were the first studies and teachings of thoughts manifesting into reality, and he turned his health around.

Since that time, there have been hundreds of essays, books, experiments, and teachings on the subject. Two of these are best-selling books of all time: *Think and Grow Rich* (1937) by Napoleon Hill and *You Can Heal Your Life* (1984) by Louise Hay. The Law of Attraction gained even more popularity in 2006 through the movie *The Secret* and was developed into a book in 2007.

You may even want to consider the Law of Attraction for your Higher Power if you are having a hard time finding something to believe in. It's most definitely extraordinarily powerful.

So, do not wallow in your pity, do not think you are incapable of recovery, do not see others that get it and believe you cannot. This is all negative conditioning you have taught yourself; your self-limiting beliefs, opinions about yourself that inhibit you from success, which are absolutely changeable. Essentially, self-limiting beliefs are your excuses as to why you stay stuck and the reasoning for your lack of willingness to even try to change. If you change your mindset, you will change those self-limiting beliefs, and a world of possibility will open up for you.

There is a three-step process to make these changes. Napoleon Hill coined this phrase in 1937 when he wrote *Think and Grow Rich*, "Whatever the mind of man can conceive and believe, the mind can achieve." And, there are your three steps: conceive, believe, and achieve.

Writing Exercise

☐ *What self-sabotaging thoughts do you tell yourself?*

☐ *What is the talk track that plays in your head?*

☐ *What are the thoughts you are attending to?*

☐ *What can you tell yourself to change the direction for your thoughts from negative to positive? What are some positive things you can tell yourself to start retraining your brain?*

☐ *What are some things you have to be grateful for? (These are important to write down and have available when you are sure there is nothing to be grateful for.)*

☐ *What are your thoughts attracting into your life?*

☐ *What are your self-limiting beliefs that keep you stuck?*

CHAPTER 18 –
CONCEIVE

What you think, you become.
What you feel, you attract.
What you imagine, you create.
-Buddha

All achievements, of any kind, were once a thought, just a dream. It all starts with the idea of a desired outcome. If your desired outcome is to live a life free from your addiction, it merely starts with the idea of it. It is that simple to start. You know others have done it. You at least know I have done it, so conceive it happening for you. There has to be a strong, deep-rooted desire to be clean and sober or to abstain from your addiction, whatever that might be.

You will not get there by trying for someone else. You will not get there if you don't know it's what you want. You will not get there if you don't make a commitment to yourself and set the intent to do so. And, you will not get there if you are not willing to go to any lengths for it, just like you did to get your fix.

Your addiction made you do crazy things for it, and most likely got you in lots of trouble because of it. You must be willing to do crazy things to stay clear from it, too. That might mean calling your sponsor in the middle of the night instead of your drug dealer. It might mean driving two hours to get to a meeting or convention instead of to get your fix. It might mean staying later at your job to avoid the happy hour crowd. It might mean finding new places to hang out and new people to hang out with. It could mean all kinds of good-for-you, crazy things.

Start envisioning what your life will look like living happy, joyous, and free. Think about how it will feel when you're not held hostage by your addiction any longer. Visualize how your relationships will be mended, your health repaired, and your finances put back in order. It all starts with a thought, an idea of what you want, and having the faith you need to do it.

Jim Rohn says, "Faith is the ability to see things that don't yet exist. If you cannot see it when it's not here then it will never be here." Take for example if you want to build a house. Of course you can see it before it exists. You design it and make a plan for it. In fact, you wouldn't even consider starting to build it before the plan exists. The sooner you design your new life, the sooner you will start living it.

Take this metaphor. Close your eyes and imagine yourself sitting in a beautiful theatre with a large screen in front of you. Play a movie of yourself living the life of your dreams. Watch it unfold as you do the things you want to do in the places you want to be with the people you want to be with. This is a visualization exercise in creating the best you. Do this as often as you can, everyday, every hour if need be, and you will manifest it into existence.

Your subconscious mind doesn't know the difference between your imagination and your reality. Your brain interprets the world around you by the images your eyes see. When you close your eyes and imagine, your brain understands it to be exactly the same as if you were seeing it in reality. This is why the placebo effect works over and over in every application, because of The Law of Attraction; what you think about, comes about.

So start by conceiving your new life.

Writing Exercise

(Be as detailed as possible.)

☐ *What is your desired outcome for your life?*

☐ *What lengths are you willing to go to for your recovery?*

☐ *Where are the places you will hang out?*

☐ *Who are the people you will surround yourself with?*

☐ *How will you spend your time?*

CHAPTER 19 -
BELIEVE

"Whether you think you can or whether you think you can't,
you're right."
-Henry Ford

Start believing in yourself. I don't care what your circumstances are; I don't care where you come from or how bad you have it. I can direct you to hundreds of books and stories of people who had it worse and made good. People born in poverty, beaten down or beaten up, people who never stood a chance in life if it weren't for their mindset and belief system.

You have to have the faith in yourself to know you can do it. You will one hundred percent self-sabotage if you don't believe in yourself. All the excuses and negative thoughts have to be diffused and thrown out of your head. This is when "stop, cancel, clear, get the fuck (or fear) out of here" comes into play. The self-doubt will come into your mind—it's a habit of your brain, but get rid of it as soon as it does, change your thought, and start paving the road to a new habit.

I talked earlier of positive affirmations. You may have thought they were dumb or silly, but they are not. They are essential to your recovery. Your brain is full of negative affirmations, and they need to be replaced with positive ones, so you had better start thinking positively about positive affirmations.

I'm thinking about Muhammad Ali as I write about positive affirmations. His affirmation was so simple yet so strong, you can't think of him without thinking of it. "I am the greatest." He said this long before he was ever the greatest. His positive thinking and belief in himself are classic examples that positive affirmations work and thoughts become things. Again, positive energies attract positive energies.

A positive mindset is key to believing in yourself. You have to trust, with absolute resolution: you have the power within yourself to make this change.

You must have a definiteness of purpose and a burning desire to recover. Oftentimes in life, this is called your "why." This is not a hope or wish; it is a conviction. Don't have a wishbone where you ought to have a backbone. You must have confidence in your ability to recover, and you must overcome your fears in order to make it happen. Here's another thing FEAR stands for: Fuck Everything And Run. And for you, that means running right back to your fix of choice. It's not an option.

So, you must stand in the face of your fears and stare them down. Nothing is so scary that you cannot live through it. Think about that. I'm sure by this point you've lived through some pretty scary stuff. Things you rightly should have feared, things others would literally have run from in fear. I can promise you, if you've made it this far, you can get through your fears of giving up your fix of choice and of recovery.

You cannot let your shame or guilt get the best of you, you cannot let what others think of you cloud your belief in yourself, nor can you get caught up in what you have done in the past. You must convince yourself this can all be overcome. And if you have to, "fake it till you make it" or "act as if." Your brain won't know the difference. In time, as Napoleon Hill implies, by demanding persistence of yourself and continuous action towards this attainment, it will come to fruition. You just have to believe.

Writing Exercise

- ☐ *What are some positive thoughts you can tell yourself?*

- ☐ *Come up with some short, positive affirmations you can tell yourself when the negative comes in.*

- ☐ *What is your why; what is your burning desire?*

- ☐ *What are some of the things you can start believing in yourself?*

- ☐ *What are some things in your life you can overcome?*

- ☐ *How can you fake it till you make it?*

CHAPTER 20 –
ACHIEVE

"Anything is possible once you believe you are worthy of achieving it."
- Jason Pockrandt

Because of the Universal Law of Attraction, what you think about and believe in comes about. With that being said, as you sit today, you are an accumulation of what you think and believe about yourself. You are a sum of the choices you have made to date because of your beliefs. You have no one to blame for your situation other than yourself.

Earl Nightingale said it like this, "We are all self-made, but only the successful admit it."

Perhaps we wouldn't have chosen some of our circumstances given the option, but we all have the choice of decision in what we do about it.

We are all put on this earth with free will. In fact, human beings are the only ones put here with free will. We are the only species that can alter the course of our lives. We are not governed by instinct or genetic code; what a shame if you don't use this to your advantage.

You can blubber all you want about your parents and the dysfunctional home you grew up in, but you're not alone. In fact, according to the late John Bradshaw, family dynamics expert, research has shown ninety-six percent of all families have some degree of dysfunction whereby the families' interactions are distorted by the addictions and compulsions of one or more members.

So, get over the blame game. You're part of the majority, welcome to the world. It's not your parents, significant other, kids, relatives, or friends; they have no control over you or what you do. You are the only one responsible for your life and the decisions in it. It's time to take responsibility for where you are in every aspect of your life. You have all the power, giving it away to others is just selfish on your part; it's your way of having someone else to blame when things go wrong.

When you conceive, by imagining and dreaming of a different way of living, you believe wholeheartedly, without a shadow of a doubt that you have the capability to attain it and you retrain your brain with positive thoughts and reinforcement, the Law of Attraction has to deliver.

Just as gravity keeps you planted on the earth or magnetism creates electrical currents that attract or repel, your thoughts and belief system about yourself will manifest into who you are and what you will become. These are physical laws. They cannot be seen, felt, touched, or smelled, but they exist. Once you understand how the Law of Attraction works in your life, your potential is endless.

Let me give you some idea of what I'm referring to here.

Take Roger Banister for example. In 1954, no one had ever run a mile in less than four minutes. Doctors and neurologists said it was impossible for human legs to run that fast, and that it could be deadly for those that tried.

Roger Banister did not believe that. He had the mindset that he could do it. And on May 6, 1954, he ran the mile in 3:59:4, unlocking the door to what was possible. As long as it took to break that barrier, it only took forty-six days for his record to be broken. Roger Banister changed what was once thought impossible.

Just as Henry Ford did with the automobile, Thomas Edison did with electricity, and Steve Jobs did with Apple, you merely have to conceive what you want to achieve, set the intention of making it so, and believe it is possible. Then this universal law takes over, and whatever that conception is, it will be delivered.

So, if you're not, as of today, a subscriber to the Law of Attraction, how would you explain people achieving what was once thought impossible? How would you provide justification for so many inventions and dreams coming true? And, most importantly, what have you got to lose by trying it on?

Darren Hardy says it like this, "It has been proven countless times by average people with meager beginnings who have risen to become extraordinary, world-changing achievers: anything you can clearly visualize and genuinely desire is within the realm of possibility for you."

If you think it's impossible for you to rid yourself of your active addiction, think again. It's just another excuse. Look around you; clearly, anything is attainable.

Writing Exercise

- ☐ *Were there circumstances that made you believe you had no free will?*

- ☐ *What decisions did you make or not make because you thought you were a victim of those circumstances?*

- ☐ *Do you blame others for where you are in your life?*

- ☐ *Do you understand you only have yourself to blame; it always comes back to your responsibility?*

- ☐ *What are some examples of what your thoughts have brought into your life?*

CHAPTER 21 –
YOU ARE WHAT YOU EAT

"You are what you eat, so don't be fast, easy, cheap, or fake."
-Unknown

We talked about addiction leaving the addict bankrupt in body, mind, and spirit. Recovery is the process of restoring the balance of all three. You cannot leave one out of balance, or the "warning signs" will start showing up, being just a matter of time until relapse occurs.

I've addressed the mind; having to change your mindset, limiting beliefs, attitude of gratitude, etc. I've addressed the spirit; having to find a higher power, something greater than yourself to believe in, that self-willing it does not work. Now let's talk about healing the body.

Earlier I mentioned the work being done in the area of addiction nutrition. I met with Victoria Abel, MA, MNT, CAN, Addiction Nutritionist and owner of Center for Addiction Nutrition in Prescott, Arizona, in an effort to help you understand how important healing the body is to recovery.

The research being done in this field is outstanding. With the implementation of proper nutrition through whole foods and supplements, the rate of success in recovery can increase by thirty-eight percent! Here's why. We all know about the brain in the head and what it's responsible for, but how many of us are familiar with the gut brain? There is a second brain located in your belly that's responsible for way more than you give it credit for. As Mark David, author of Nourishing Wisdom, says, "It's called a gut feeling not an elbow feeling for a reason."

The gut brain or belly brain refers to the gastrointestinal (GI) tract. The GI tract consists of your esophagus, stomach, large and small intestines and is where you break down and absorb food. There are actually brain-like cells in the GI tract that act similarly to brain cells in the head. Yes, you have a second brain. Just as important as what you feed your mind is what you feed your belly.

All trauma, addiction, and mood disorders impact the body, and the body manifests it psychologically. You've all heard of dopamine and serotonin. These are the chemicals produced in our bodies that are affected by addiction. I'm sure you've heard of these in connection with the chemistry in your brain. Here's what you haven't heard; dopamine and serotonin are produced in the gut! Only five to ten percent of these chemicals are actually in the brain at a time, the other ninety to ninety-five percent is stored in your gut.

What this means for you as an addict is that it's imperative you heal the gut. This is the field of Gut Microbiota. There are over 1,000 types of bacteria in your belly, as individual to a person as their DNA, and this bacteria in your gut is constantly talking with your brain. Because addiction kills off the good bacteria and feeds the less beneficial or bad bacteria, your body does not produce dopamine and serotonin naturally, you become dependent on the fix to do it. This means cravings and needing more and more.

Sugar becomes an addiction to many recovering addicts because it is the only food that constantly releases dopamine to the brain. And although suggested as an alternative to other addictive behaviors, even in the Big Book of Alcoholics Anonymous, it is not the answer. Sugar is just another addiction for the body. By changing the microbiota of the gut through proper nutrition, again with whole foods and supplements, the problem—not just the symptoms—can be resolved.

Let's talk about the importance of whole foods. Yes, I'm talking real food, not processed, and preferably organic foods, but I'm also talking about the foods that heal your gut. You may have heard of probiotics; they are great for gut health as they contain live organisms with specific strains of bacteria (think of yogurt). The problem is with 1,000 plus strains of bacteria in the gut, knowing the right strains to target becomes virtually impossible. What is different and essential with whole foods is they provide prebiotics. Prebiotics are specialized plant fibers and grains that act like fertilizers to stimulate the growth of healthy bacteria in the gut. If eating good, nutritious food is going to be new for you, start with these two simple tips: if it goes bad, it's good for you, and shop the perimeter of the grocery store.

If you're reading this book and thinking your fix of choice doesn't affect your gut microbiota because your habit isn't drugs or alcohol, maybe your fix is sex, social media, or gambling, think again.

It used to be believed that there was a difference in brain chemistry between different types of addiction. However, newer research shows that the reward pathways (talked about previously) are regulated by the addictive behavior, and it doesn't matter what the addiction is. The stimuli to the body ALL react the same in the brain. When you begin to heal the gut, dopamine is released naturally to reduce cravings and ultimately reduce relapse, no matter what the fix of choice.

Proper nutrition is also a reducer of stress and anxiety. Both trauma victims and addicts have what is called an upregulated nervous system. It's like being on high alert all the time. Think of this scenario; two people sitting in a quiet cafe, one with an upregulated nervous system and one with a normal nervous system. Someone comes in and the wind slams the door shut. The person with the upregulated system is going to freak out, jump out of the seat, and look for where the trouble is. The normal person turns towards the door and thinks, "Oh it's windy." An upregulated nervous system raises the bad bacteria in the gut. Addressing proper nutrition, again rebuilding the good bacteria, downregulates the nervous system, lessening stress and anxiety.

Victoria explains that it is extremely helpful to identify not only the addict's fix of choice but also the feeling they get because of it. Whether bringing up from a depressed state, getting an in utero type of floating feeling, having euphoria, experiencing numbing, establishing a connection with spirit, or perceiving other significant feelings associated with using, she can understand what they need nutritionally or for their brain chemistry to heal. This allows her to target a nutritional plan with whole foods and supplements that will help balance the chemistry and support recovery.

Truly the science of Addictionology and Addiction Nutrition is outstanding in identifying how to heal the body in recovery. Victoria is one of the pioneers in this field, is a kick-ass woman, and is doing amazing things in the addiction world. I recommend you visit her website for so much more information: www.centerforaddictionnutrition.com.

The other thing I want to mention in this chapter that Victoria stresses to her clients is this: "The food you eat mirrors your life." Think about that. The food you eat is a direct reflection of how you feel about yourself, your self worth. If you're not eating much at all, eating out of a dumpster, or eating dollar meals at McDonalds, this is all the worth you are giving to your life. If you want to see the value you place on yourself, look at your food choices. Changing your choices of food will not only improve your chances of recovery, it will change your life.

Writing Exercise - These are the five questions Victoria would ask if you were her client:

☐ *How do you fantasize about food?*

☐ *How do you gather what you need?*

☐ *How do you make your food?*

☐ *How do you eat your food?*

☐ *How do you clean up after your food?*

CHAPTER 22 –
THE RULES OF RECOVERY

"Success is nothing more than a few simple disciplines practiced every day."
-Jim Rohn

In Chapter 2, I gave you the Rules of Addiction, what is required of an addict. When you make the decision to move from active addiction to recovery, in turn, there are going to be rules of recovery. Think of these as the ingredients in the recipe of recovery. These are the things to keep in check at all times, the things that will keep you from relapsing. Play by these rules.

> **Rule 1.** *Be honest.* Stop hiding shit. As Alcoholics Anonymous teaches, recovery means being honest in all of your affairs. Your secrets keep you sick, so you must not keep secrets. Getting and staying honest with yourself, as well as those in your life, is essential to your recovery.
>
> **Rule 2.** *Practice humility.* I'll remind you; it's not thinking less of yourself, but thinking about yourself less. Being of service to others will go a long way in your journey to humility. Find activities and situations where you can practice being humble.
>
> **Rule 3.** *Forgive.* You must learn to forgive yourself and the people you've been blaming for the problems in your life. Being unable to forgive, especially yourself, will keep you stuck. You must forgive to grow, and you have to let it go.

Rule 4. *Find a higher power.* You must find something greater than yourself to believe in. Whether you find it in God, a spirit, the fellowship of others, or some other form is irrelevant, but it is essential. Believing in something outside yourself will give you the power, strength, knowledge, etc. to make a difference in your life and keep you from your ineffective efforts of self-willing it.

Rule 5. *Adopt a Positive Mindset.* Feed the right wolf. Stomp out negative thoughts and emotions by figuring out a way to chase them away when they enter your mind. And they will, so be prepared with a way to shoot them down. Focus on the positive, all the good things you're doing and accomplishing. It's a process and you need to be gentle with yourself along the way as you change your mindset from the negative to the positive. Remember these are old habits you are replacing, and developing new habits takes time and consistency.

Rule 6. Have an *Attitude of Gratitude.* Find ways to be grateful everyday; maybe it's by keeping a gratitude journal or showing random acts of kindness to the people around you. Maybe it's through meditation or prayer. It doesn't matter which way you choose to show gratitude, just make sure you do.

Rule 7. *Be of service to others.* This is how you change from selfish to selfless. Be accountable. Pop back into the places where your recovery started to show others the way. Get outside yourself and find ways others might need you and where you can help.

Rule 8. *Always be conceiving, believing, and achieving.* Don't get complacent. Constantly set goals and do the work to attain them. Use these three concepts over and over again in your life to create anything you desire.

Rule 9. *Stop romanticizing your using.* This is counterproductive to recovery. Your using days were not ideal or heroic. Those days are over, and really, they weren't all that great. Rather, start idealizing recovery and the freedom from being held hostage by your addiction.

Rule 10. *Avoid tempting situations.* Stay away from the places where you used and the people you used with. These people and places are memory triggers, and by avoiding them, you are avoiding the chance of relapse. Remember as addicts, we can handle anything but temptation, so, don't put yourself in temptation's way.

Rule 11. *Don't isolate.* Keep a positive network of friends and associations. Keep an active schedule and stick to it. Don't slide on your responsibilities and obligations to your schedule. Talk about your feelings and emotions; don't bottle it up inside.

Rule 12. *Stick to your aftercare plan.* If it's going to meetings, therapy sessions, groups, taking medication, or whatever else your plan consists of, don't deviate. Once you get off track, you will find it easier and easier to do it more often, so keep up the good work and commitments.

Rule 13. *Watch what you eat.* Stop eating shit (all processed foods). Do not feed yourself with foods that will deplete your body of what it needs. Keep your cravings at bay by keeping your gut balanced to produce its own dopamine and serotonin. Remember you are what you eat and whatever else you put into your body as well.

Rule 14. *Don't pick up/use/go back to your fix of choice.* Don't misguide yourself thinking you can handle this even once. You cannot. Pick up the phone instead; call someone that can help. Do what it takes at all costs to not do it, even once.

Rule 15. *If you find yourself fixating on something new, seek help.* As addicts we tend to look for the next best thing to make us feel good. When you find yourself obsessing or fixating on something new, it's possible you're heading towards a cross-addiction. Seek help, talk to someone, and do not keep it a secret. Left unattended, it will lead you back to your fix of choice.

CHAPTER 23 –
DISRUPTING THE POWER OF OBSESSIVE THINKING

"Thoughts are just fleeting mental images. They have no consequences until you choose to make them important."
-Deepak Chopra

Just as in active addiction, there will be times in recovery when your fix of choice will consume you and take over your brain. Be prepared; obsessive or ruminating thinking will happen. Obsessive thinking is having a series of negative thoughts or judgments without the ability to gain control over them, whereas ruminating thinking is comprised of repetitive thoughts that cause feelings of sadness or distress. Both can be utterly debilitating. Trying not to think about negative, obsessive thoughts is nearly impossible once they creep in. It's like trying not to think about a pink elephant when someone says, "Don't think about a pink elephant." It's the exact thing our brain will think of next. Instead of simply being told what not to do, our brains need replacement activities or tools.

Let's talk about the tools you can use when your brain sucks you into these thought obsessions. I say "thought" obsessions because that's all they are, just thoughts, thoughts that you don't have to act on, thoughts that will go away, and thoughts that will eventually make you stronger in recovery.

1. Simply ask your higher power to remove the obsession, over and over, until it's removed.

2. Use Andy Dooley's "Stop, cancel, clear, get the fuck (or fear) out of here."

3. Use breathing techniques. Breathe in, bringing fresh, positive thoughts, to the count of four and breathe out negative energy and thoughts to the count of four.

4. Pick up the phone and talk to someone to get your mind onto something else.

5. Write down the thoughts and examine them. What triggers them? How do you respond to them?

6. Accept them; you can even make them your friends. Welcome them back, appreciate them for visiting, and then politely ask them to leave.

7. Ground yourself by planting your feet firmly on the ground and take in your surroundings using all your senses.

8. Engage in exercise of any kind. Take a walk out the front door if that's all you have accessible.

9. Use meditation and mindfulness techniques. (Something you'll have to learn about if you are interested.)

10. LOL... laugh out loud. Every time we laugh, our brains release dopamine automatically making us feel happier, helping to relieve obsessive thoughts. So, be a dope and just randomly start laughing! Or watch a sitcom or go to a comedy show.

11. SOL... sing out loud. Musical vibrations change the brain and lower levels of hormones associated with obsessive thinking.

12. Be social. Get outside yourself and be with others.

13. Practice being grateful. Each negative thought has an equal or opposite thought; practice thoughts of gratefulness.

14. Try the old rubber band on the wrist and snap it every time obsessive thoughts show up.

CHAPTER 24 –
FINDING MY REDEMPTION

"Make peace with your past.
Otherwise it will screw up the present and your future."
-Jim Rohn

Prison gave me the time away I needed to figure some shit out. Sure, I could have used that sentence to be bitter, resentful, and antagonistic. I saw plenty of guys in there sneaking contraband: cell phones, cigarettes, drugs, and there was plenty of gambling going on. I could have been that guy. The arrogant, "I'll show them" kind of guy, but once again, I realized if my best thinking had gotten me here, maybe it's time to listen. If I don't have my best interest in mind, maybe I'll defer to someone that does.

And so I used my time wisely. I went back to the basics, drew on what I had learned previously when I had been clean and sober. I found humility again. Believe me, it wasn't hard under the circumstances. But I stopped thinking so much of myself and thought about others.

I started a weekly recovery meeting in prison. It was three guys and myself. We'd sit at a picnic table, the four of us, with an agenda to share our experience of what brought us together, our strength in how we were getting through, and the hope for our futures. We attracted attention from others seeking fellowship, vitality, and encouragement from our group. Eventually we were given a room to hold our meeting, and it grew to over forty to fifty people serving both inmates and those from the community around us.

I taught classes in prison on public speaking and business, and they were the most well-attended classes in the history of the prison. I was one of four inmates chosen out of the 1,000 there to speak, along with another inmate of my choice, outside the prison to high schools and colleges in the area on business ethics and addiction. I was also asked to be a liaison between the staff and inmates to facilitate RDAP (Residential Drug Abuse Program), a cognitive behavior therapy program for incarcerated addicts.

When I make my life about others, I come to life. Since addiction is a selfish disease, the antidote is getting outside oneself and being selfless. When I come from a selfless frame of mind, it's so much easier to keep my addictions in check. These are the simple things I can do. Again, it's not hard; it's easy to do, but easy not to do.

I spent thirty-six months in Federal Prison Camp in Duluth, MN and came out with my fourth nickname, Emmis 36. I spent my time thinking about the life I wanted to live upon my release, how I would conduct myself. I had disappointed most everyone in my life and ruined a lot of those lives financially and emotionally. I would be fifty-seven years old when I got out, and I had nothing; I would literally be starting over.

Coming out of prison was emotionally the hardest thing I have ever done. I couldn't have imagined the lows it would take me to. I had the option of living in a halfway house or "at home," except I didn't have a home. During my prison sentence, my ex-wife had lost both our homes to foreclosure. She was now renting a home that had never been mine. Because of the kids, she let me move in, but I felt like a complete stranger.

I didn't want to see anyone, I didn't want to make any connections on the outside, and I wasn't comfortable. I didn't know how people would respond to me. I was depressed, and life on the outside was now overwhelming.

Adding to my low emotional state was my inability to get a good night's sleep. I was so accustomed to the lights and commotion all night in prison. I couldn't sleep, even with a light and TV on. I was also awakened at random times twice each night by the Bureau of Federal Prisons, part of the process in being allowed to be home rather than a halfway house. I would have to call back with a specific code to ensure them I was where I was supposed to be. With the lack of sleep and emotions running high, it was all I could do to focus on anything positive.

I had put all my thoughts, for so long, into just getting out of prison; I never considered what it might be like. I was sure the pure joy of being out would provide happiness. Clearly that wasn't the case.

I had to report to the halfway house two times a week and finish the treatment plan I had started in prison, meeting with my counselor twice a week. I was told to get a job, but because of my crimes, I couldn't have any financial responsibility. That meant no access to anyone's credit card, no taking in money, not even working a cash register at McDonalds. I got a job at Goodwill, driving a forklift in the warehouse and receiving drive-through donations. Backbreaking work as I unloaded boxes, crates, furniture, and the like for eight hours a day.

As it turns out, it was exactly where I needed to be for my recovery.

As I came to and came around, I started reaching out to old friends and going to my old AA meetings. Making those connections proved to have stunning positive effects. There were those, of course, that had little interest in hearing from me, but for the most part I was well received and thought of. My fears of being an outcast to society, of being unwelcome with the people and places that had once made up my life, were unfounded. Once again, proving nine out of ten times our fears never come to pass.

After six months at Goodwill, my probation officer let me take a job working for a friend of mine in business development for his construction company. Though these were jobs that gave me a paycheck, my true focus was finding my redemption. I nurtured my thoughts on helping others, making a difference in the lives of addicts and having a positive impact on the opioid epidemic in our country.

I also had a new personal interest in helping those like me, who were facing prison time and had no idea what to expect. From investigations, indictment, pre-sentencing, and prison time to acclimating back to the outside, I felt I could help others navigate through the experience.

I journaled for the first sixty days when I got out of prison and was later asked to turn those writings over to my probation officer. They are now used as a guide to help others and determine their progress coming out of prison. I've made contacts with criminal attorneys and worked as a Prison Consultant on protocol to help those going in or coming out of prison.

I talked with and listened to anyone and everyone who worked in the field of recovery or the opioid epidemic in our country. I went to every seminar and conference and listened to every speaker on the topic. I networked at the weekend-long Twin Cities Film Festival where the FBI introduced their program, Chasing The Dragon, a film and program to introduce Minnesotan schools to the prevention and awareness of opioid addiction. I engaged with Tonka Cares, a prevention-focused coalition working with the FBI, DEA, local law enforcement, businesses, city government, and Minnetonka Public Schools to support positive decision-making among young people.

I started speaking on addiction and recovery every chance I got and sponsored as many addicts as I could fit into my schedule. I have connected with Hazelden Betty Ford and speak on a continuing basis at their numerous facilities. To this day, I attend at least four AA meetings a week and surround myself with likeminded people.

I've put together a prevention and awareness program for school-aged kids and continue to develop that mission. I became a Nationally Certified Intervention Specialist and a Nationally Certified Recovery Coach and am on Hazelden Betty Ford's list of preferred providers.

I've connected with the opioid panel in the state of Minnesota, and I work on the board of advocacy for the Steve Rummler Hope Network, lobbying against big pharmaceutical companies and helping to create legislation for the HF400 Opioid Product Stewardship Bill. This bill will require large pharmaceutical companies to contribute a small amount of their profits to address the opioid epidemic in our country and help pay for prevention and treatment of those affected.

I am also working on a video series with Twin Cities PBS in St. Paul. It is their mission to launch a statewide prevention and education campaign on the opioid crisis in Minnesota.

I was approached to help open a treatment center in Somerset, WI, a project I am most proud of. The Lodge on St. Croix is a non-profit and will offer an alternate, affordable way of treatment. As I write this, we are working with an engineer on planning and approval with the township and county.

My relationships with my two daughters, ages twenty-one and twenty-three, are better than any one of us could have imagined. I am proud to say they call me their best friend and though one lives just fifteen miles away and the other in another state, I talk to each of them at least once a day (oftentimes a half a dozen). I am making up for the lost time with them that my addictions and prison took away. They are my inspiration.

My ex-wife and I still live together. We make great roommates, and we are the best of friends. Though we know it's only temporary, it works perfectly for us right now. And as I'm sure you've figured out by now, we collaborated to write this book together. We are also working on a nonfiction book chronicling my story and our lives together as addict and "normie."

And, most important to my recovery and my well being, I pay my restitution on a monthly basis to those I financially harmed.

Today I find happiness through clean living. The way I feel today is the way I always looked to my fixes to make me feel. I always thought the next big money deal, drug high, or gambling win would fix me, make everything better. I had to lose everything to see that the key to happiness was inside me and in my control the whole time.

Today my insides match my outsides. Today I don't subscribe to other esteem; I get it from being the best me I can be. Today the outside "stuff" isn't what I need to fill me up; those things were just signs of my unhappiness within. Today I nurture the inside, not the outside. Today I am comfortable in my own skin and do not need others' approval; as long as I am doing what I'm suppose to, I approve of myself. Today I have self-esteem.

It's been two and a half years since I got out of prison, four years since I have gambled and eight years since I kicked my opioid and heroin addictions. I know I will always have another use in me—I am not immune to a relapse—but I don't know if I have another recovery. For today I am not willing to see if the revolving door still works.

When I take off my shoes at the end of the day, I bend down to tuck them away and thank my higher power for another day of abstinence. When I put them on each morning, I ask for one more day. For now it's one day at a time. At other times, it's one hour at a time or even one minute at a time, but I've come to learn that's how recovery works.

This is what recovery looks like for me. For each recovering addict, it will be different, but the ingredients will be similar. Take your recovery on like you did your addiction; put that kind of attention, willingness, thought, money, and whatever else you threw at your addiction into it. Go to those lengths to recover, and you will have an extraordinary life. Invest in yourself rather than your addiction; you're worth it. And, investing in yourself shows others you are worth it, too.

Look, I know I've given you a great deal of information to digest; even taking it one day at a time, I realize it's a lot. But you cannot be overwhelmed by the work it will take to recover and dismiss it. It's one step at a time, something to work at everyday. Take this scenario. If your life depended on you getting out of a thirty-story burning building, and the only way out was to the roof, and the only way to the roof was the stairs; you do not look at the top of thirty stories of stairs. That would be overwhelming. You put your head down and take one stair at a time to save your life. Abstaining from your fix of choice works the same way. Don't look at how far you have to go, just take one step at a time, one day at a time. Your life does depend on it.

We, the addicted, are some of the most powerful, creative, intelligent, loveable, though at times misguided people on the planet. Get it right and you can create a happy ending to your story.

My hope for everyone that reads this book is that you get it, keep it, and have the chance, like I've had, to give it away. But, unfortunately my hope isn't enough; you have to have hope. With it, however, lives are transformed, families repaired, friendships mended, and redemption found.

GET INVOLVED

There are a lot of David's out there working tirelessly to bring the opioid epidemic to an end. But, there are a lot more needed. If you want to get involved with helping the cause, here are some of the important changes that need to happen and where you can make a difference.

Addicts need a voice and not one with a stigma attached. Unfortunately, the negative connotation just in the word itself has a self-defeating impact. Be a part of the movement into recovery, whether getting there yourself or helping a loved one get there.

The more lives that can be turned around and the more successes that come out of it, the more that stigma will change. Just imagine a world where an addict is thought of as a passionate, focused, smart, diligent, and dedicated person at whatever it is they put their mind to. When we change the number of addicts getting into treatment, upwards of fifty percent rather than the eleven percent it stands at, the negative connotation will be combated. Changing the context to "being addicted to recovery and success" sure would change the way people thought about the word "addict."

With the lack of funding for treatment for those who can't afford it, treatment is prohibitive. To change the numbers of those seeking treatment, there has to be funding available. The big pharmaceutical companies that created the problem in the first place need to be held accountable. Bills like HF400 or Penny A Pill Bill have to be pushed through each state, forcing these companies to pay the state a percentage of their profits from the business they do in that state. You can get involved with your local and state legislators to advocate and lobby for these causes.

Addiction treatment services need to be covered by all insurance companies. Every individual that needs treatment should be afforded that opportunity without the chance of denial. Again, seek out your local representatives to advocate for change.

Data from a national study of state and federal prisons showed that sixty-three to eighty-three percent of arrestees had drugs in their system at the time of arrest. Throughout the system, more than sixty-five percent of the prison population meets medical criteria for substance abuse addiction. We are the largest incarcerated country in the world and almost three-fourths of that population has an addiction issue. I can't say how many, but I'll bet an awful lot of these people need treatment not incarceration. Again, treatment needs to be accessible to everyone.

One of the most important places to advocate for change is in our schools. It is imperative that prevention and awareness programs be implemented. Addiction education is just as important as sex education, and that starts in schools as early as fourth and fifth grades. Kids are going to be offered drugs and alcohol as early as they're going to be introduced to sexual opportunities, so why aren't we preparing them? If we don't get to them that early, it will be too late. Kids need to understand what they are up against and the tools to navigate around it.

States are trying to stay away from mandating curriculum because they are at a loss as to how to handle it. But it needs to be handled. School districts don't know what to do, so nothing is being done. Grade- and age-specific curriculum needs to be developed, modeled, and replicated throughout the country with clear-cut goals in mind.

For more information on how you can be the difference for effective change, contact your local representatives and legislators. If David can be of help in answering your questions or giving you direction on how to help these causes, please reach out to him at David@TheLifeRecoveryCoach. com. He will respond to you within twenty-four hours.

ABOUT THE AUTHORS

David Marion has been a motivational speaker for twenty-nine years. He has spoken his message of inspiration and hope to tens of thousands of people. Since 1989, he has helped hundreds find a life in recovery through his message, work, and sponsorship.

He is a Nationally Certified Intervention Professional and a Nationally Certified Recovery Coach.

This is his first book collaboration to bring his message of hope and recovery to more people. It is his passion to make a bigger and better impact in the world of addiction and on the opioid crisis our nation faces.

Born and raised, though never grew up (as he will tell you), on Long Island in New York, he has lived in Minnesota since 1989. Having been sent there on a one-way ticket for treatment by his parents, he has never left.

David lives with his ex-wife, Dana Golden, temporarily, as he creates his new life after a three-year federal prison stint. They are currently collaborating on a nonfiction memoir chronicling their over-the-top story of his money, drug, and gambling addictions throughout his life and their life together. When he is not helping other addicts or speaking, he spends as much time as possible with his two daughters.

Dana Golden is a serial entrepreneur, personal development seeker, and major manifester. Her passion for writing has led her to journaling throughout her life and she has written children's stories and poems, though just for her family. This is her first book, and she is excited to bring her passion to fruition.

Dana has been on the other side of addiction as a codependent and enabler since she was a child to an addicted parent. She grew up in Columbus, Ohio, and after eight years in Los Angeles, California, moved to Minnesota to be closer to her only sister.

Most of all, she adores being the mother to her two daughters. She lives with her ex-husband, David Marion, as he navigates his journey since being incarcerated and finds his redemption. She looks forward to bringing you their next book collaboration.

How to reach David

No matter where you are in your journey, David Marion can help you, in life and recovery. David's specialties range from leading planned interventions to sober coaching to repairing families that have been torn apart by addiction.

If you or someone you know is struggling with addiction, there is hope. If you don't know where to start or even the questions to ask, David does. Whether it's getting into treatment, a program of recovery, or an assessment of the situation, he wants to hear from you. Don't hesitate; don't wait; he welcomes you to reach out to him at David@TheLifeRecoveryCoach. com.

Every addict's path is different, and determining that path is essential to successful recovery. Having an expert such as David is crucial. With the multitude of resources and tools out there, without an expert on your side to navigate through the throngs of options, it can be overwhelming. David can set you in the right direction to recovering your body, mind, and spirit.

David is a motivational speaker, available to speak throughout the world on addiction and recovery. His story is powerful, filled with highs, lows, and everything in between. He keeps audiences of all ages and backgrounds engaged and wanting more with his passionate message. From business or school audiences, to conventions and drug and alcohol panels,

David's story will lift you up, bring you hope, inspire, and teach about the importance of every choice we make.

If you want to connect with David, simply shoot him an email at David@TheLifeRecoveryCoach.com and he will get back to you the same day.

Please visit his website for more information on David and his expertise. www.TheLifeRecoveryCoach.com

TEAR OUT SHEETS

The next five pages are tear sheets for you to use as reminders. Tear them out, keep them handy, and refer to them often.

Use the "Rules of Addiction" page to remind you of the havoc your addiction reaps in your life.

Use the "All Your Excuses" page to keep yourself in check. If you're saying these things to yourself or others, you're in denial. Be one hundred percent honest in all your affairs and see these excuses for what they are, a way to keep you sick and stuck.

Use the "Rules of Recovery" page to make sure you're doing the right things and staying engaged in your recovery.

Use the "Warning Signs of Relapse" page to make sure you're not falling into stinking thinking or checking out of life and into your addictive behaviors.

Use the "Disrupting the Power of Obsessive Thinking" page when you find yourself stuck in your own head spiraling with obsessive or ruminating thoughts.

RULES OF ADDICTION

The things your disease requires of you that hold you hostage.

1. Your addiction requires you to use the stuff whether it's killing you or those around you.

2. Your addiction dictates where you hang out and who you hang out with.

3. You cannot control it once you start.

4. You don't get to finish anything you start.

5. Addiction kicks potential's ass.

6. Addiction is a selfish disease.

7. Addiction is a disease of loneliness and isolation

8. Addiction requires too much space in your brain.

9. Addiction will strip you of self-love and respect.

10. Addiction demands you do things you wouldn't otherwise do.

11. Addiction makes you delusional.

12. Your fix of choice will require you to use/do more and more over time.

13. Addiction will rob you of your body, mind, and spirit.

14. You will suffer severe consequences.

15. Addiction, left untreated, has one of three outcomes: jails, institutions, or death.

TEAR SHEET #2
ALL YOUR EXCUSES

If you catch yourself saying these to yourself or others, there's a problem.

1. If it gets really bad, I'll quit.

2. Everyone else does it.

3. You'd do it, too, if you had my life.

4. I'm more interesting and outgoing when I do.

5. I'm not hurting anyone.

6. No one understands me or can help me.

7. I'm never going to amount to anything anyway.

8. This is who I am; I'm ok with it.

9. I can stop whenever I want.

10. I deserve this escape.

11. I've always been the black sheep of my family.

12. It makes me better/happier.

13. I'm not as bad as him/her; now they have a problem!

14. I'm not suffering any earth-shattering consequences.

15. I don't drink (or whatever your fix is) that much.

16. I only do it on the weekends.

17. I don't go at it hard-core or use the hard-core stuff.

18. The universe is always conspiring against me.

RULES OF RECOVERY

Check in with yourself. Are you adhering to these principles?

1. Be honest.

2. Practice humility.

3. Forgive.

4. Find a higher power.

5. Adopt a positive mindset.

6. Have an attitude of gratitude.

7. Be of service to others.

8. Always conceive and believe to achieve.

9. Stop romanticizing your using.

10. Avoid tempting situations.

11. Don't isolate.

12. Stick to your aftercare plan.

13. Don't pick up/use or go back to your fix of choice.

14. Watch what you eat.

15. If you find yourself fixating on something new, seek help.

WARNING SIGNS OF RELAPSE

Check yourself for self-destructive signals.

1. Change in mood or behaviors.

2. Becoming intolerant, angry, or resentful.

3. Increased feeling of apathy.

4. Isolation from others.

5. Socially checking out.

6. Not going to treatment or meetings.

7. Adhering to an aftercare plan but not actively participating.

8. Not expressing emotions.

9. Change of eating or sleeping habits.

10. Lapse in taking care of oneself mentally or physically.

11. Not being grateful in recovery.

12. Being in denial.

13. Relaxing of self-imposed rules.

14. Cravings for the fix of choice.

15. Thinking about the people and places associated with using.

16. Romanticizing past using behavior rather than remembering the pain it caused.

17. Minimizing the consequences of the addiction.

18. Bargaining with yourself.

19. Lying to others.

20. Thoughts on how to better control using.

21. Planning a relapse or looking for opportunities to use.

DISRUPTING THE POWER OF OBSESSIVE THINKING

When you find yourself obsessing or ruminating, try these.

1. Simply ask your higher power to remove the obsession.

2. Use Andy Dooley's "Stop, cancel, clear, get the fuck (or fear) out of here."

3. Use breathing techniques.

4. Pick up the phone and talk to someone.

5. Write down the thoughts and examine them.

6. Accept the thoughts and make them your friends.

7. Ground yourself by planting your feet firmly on the ground.

8. Engage in exercise of any kind. Take a walk.

9. Use meditation and mindfulness techniques.

10. LOL… laugh out loud.

11. SOL… sing out loud.

12. Be social. Get outside yourself and be with others.

13. Practice being grateful.

14. Snap a rubber band on your wrist.

REFERENCES

American Society of Addiction Medicine. **https://www.asam.org/asam-home-page**

Anderson, D. J., J.P McGovern, and R.L. DuPont. 1999. "The origins of the Minnesota model of addiction treatment: A first person account." *Journal of Addictive Diseases* 18 (1): 107-114.

Ashwood Recovery at Northpoint. 2017. "How Do I Know if I'm Really an Addict?" https://www.ashwoodrecovery.com/blog/how-do-i-know-if-im-really-an-addict/

Brody, Jane E. 2013. "Effective Addiction Treatment." *New York Times* https://well.blogs.nytimes.com/2013/02/04/effective-addiction-treatment/

Centers for Disease Control and Prevention. **https://www.cdc.gov**

Clear, James. "How Long Does it Actually take to Form a New Habit." **https://jamesclear.com/new-habit**

Didenko, E. and N. Pankratz. 2007. "Substance Use: Pathways to homelessness? Or a way of adapting to street life?" *Visions: BC's Mental Health and Addictions Journal* 4 (1): 9-10. **https://www.heretohelp.bc.ca/visions/housing-and-homelessness-vol4/substance-use-pathways-homelessness**

Forbes. http://www.forbes.com/sites/moneywisewomen/2012/06/19/the-cost-of-addiction-on-families/#40d01353ada4

Hamilton, David. 2011. "Do Positive People Live Longer?" https://www.huffpost.com/entry/positive-people-live-long_b_774648

Kelly, J. F., and W.L White. 2012. "Broadening the base of addiction mutual-help organizations." *Journal of Groups in Addiction & Recovery* 7 (2-4): 82-101.

Korb, Alex. 2012. "The Grateful Brain: The Neuroscience of Giving Thanks." *Psychology Today* https://www.psychologytoday.com/us/blog/prefrontal-nudity/201211/the-grateful-brain

Lally, Phillippa, Cornelia H.M. van Jaarsveld, Henry W.W. Potts, and Jane Wardle. 2009. "How are Habits Formed: Modelling Habit Formation in the Real World." *European Journal of Social Psychology https://onlinelibrary.wiley.com/doi/full/10.1002/ejsp.674*

Marlatt, G. Alan, and Dennis M.Donovan. 2005. *Relapse Prevention, Second Edition, Maintenance Strategies in the Treatment of Addictive Behaviors.*

MediaKix Influencer Marketing Agency. https://mediakix.com/#gs. h0kd2d

NBC Nightly News. https://www.nbc.com/nbc-nightly-news

National Institute on Drug Abuse. 2018. **https://www.drugabuse.gov**

National Center on Child Abuse Prevention Research. 2001. "Current trends in child abuse prevention, reporting, and fatalities: The 1999 fifty State survey. Chicago: Prevent Child Abuse America." www.preventchildabuse.org/learn_more/research_docs/1999_50_survey.pdf

National Council on Sexual Addiction Compulsivity. **http://self.gutenberg.org/articles/national_council_on_sexual_addiction_and_compulsivity**

"National Survey on Drug Use and Health." 2017. U.S. Department of Health & Human Services: SAMHSA: Substance Abuse and mental Health Services Administration. https://www.samhsa.gov/data/report/2017-nsduh-annual-national-report

North American Foundation for Gambling Addiction. 2017. "Statistics of Gambling Addiction."

Origins Behavioral Healthcare. https://www.originsrecovery.com/?msclkid=9fd96925f1511f262309357c28bf0c8e

Rehabs.com: An American Addiction Centers Resource. Recovery Brands, LLC https://www.rehabs.com

Siegel, Richard H. 2015. "The PTSD, Trauma, Addiction Connection." *The Sober World:An Award Winning National Magazine* **https://www.thesoberworld.com/2015/04/27/ptsd-trauma-addiction-connection/**

Sinha, R. 2011. "New findings on biological factors predicting addiction relapse vulnerability." *Current Psychiatry Reports* 13 (5): 398–405.

The Center for Prisoner Health and Human Rights. "Incarceration, Substance Abuse, and Addiction." https://www.prisonerhealth.org/educational-resources/factsheets-2/incarceration-substance-abuse-and-addiction/

The Fix: Addiction and Recovery, Straight Up. https://www.thefix.com/addiction

"The Strangest Secret Earl Nightingale Conant 1950's Full." **https://www.youtube.com/watch?v=IeaBfM3TdHQ**

SUGGESTED READING LIST

7 Weeks to Sobriety by Joan Mathews Larson

Atomic Habits by James Clear

Brain Maker by David Perlmutter M.D.

Breaking the Habit of Being Yourself by Dr. Joe Dispenza

Change Your Thoughts - Change Your Life by Dr. Wayne Dyer

Eating for Recovery by Molly Siple

Excuses Begone by Dr. Wayne Dyer

Forks Over Knives by Alona Pulde M.D. and Matthew Lederman M.D.

Germs in Your Gut Are Talking to Your Brain. Scientists Want to Know What They're Saying. New York Times. January, 28, 2019.

God Made Organics Not GMO's by Karen Anne VanBarneveld-Price

Grain Brain by David Perlmutter M.D.

Healing the Shame That Binds You by John Bradshaw

How To Change Your Mind by Michael Pollan

Nourishing Wisdom by Marc David

Potatoes Not Prozac by Kathleen DesMaisons Ph.D.

The 5 Second Rule by Mel Robbins

The Compound Effect by Darren Hardy

The Vitamin Cure For Alcoholism by Abram Hoffer M.D., Ph.D.

Think and Grow Rich by Napoleon Hill

You Are the Placebo by Dr. Joe Dispenza

You can heal your life by Louise Hay